THE NEW TEMPLE SHAKESPEARE

Edited by M. R. Ridley, M.A.

KING HENRY VI
SECOND PART
by William Shakespeare

London: J. M. DENT & SONS LTD.
New York: E. P. DUTTON & CO. INC.

Made in Great Britain
by
The Temple Press · Letchworth · Herts

First Published . . 1936
Last Reprinted . . 1948

PRINTED IN GREAT BRITAIN BY
MORRISON AND GIBB LTD., LONDON AND EDINBURGH

Editor's General Note

The Text. The editor has kept before him the aim of presenting to the modern reader the nearest possible approximation to what Shakespeare actually wrote. The text is therefore conservative, and is based on the earliest reliable printed text. But to avoid distraction (*a*) the spelling is modernised, and (*b*) a limited number of universally accepted emendations is admitted without comment. Where a Quarto text exists as well as the First Folio the passages which occur only in the Quarto are enclosed in square brackets [ ] and those which occur only in the Folio in brace brackets { }.

Scene Division. The rapid continuity of the Elizabethan curtainless production is lost by the 'traditional' scene divisions. Where there is an essential difference of place these scene divisions are retained. Where on the other hand the change of place is insignificant the scene division is indicated only by a space on the page. For ease of reference, however, the 'traditional' division is retained at the head of the page and in line numbering.

Notes. Passages on which there are notes are indicated by a † in the margin.

Punctuation adheres more closely than has been usual to the 'Elizabethan' punctuation of the early texts. It is often therefore more indicative of the way in which the lines were to be delivered than of their syntactical construction.

Glossaries are arranged on a somewhat novel principle, not alphabetically, but in the order in which the words or phrases occur. The editor is much indebted to Mr. J. N. Bryson for his collaboration in the preparation of the glossaries.

Preface

The Text.   The textual problem presented by the second and third parts of *Henry VI* is quite different from that presented by the first part, and greatly more complex.   In 1594 appeared a Quarto, printed by Thomas Creed for Thomas Millington, entitled: 'The First part of the Contention betwixt the two famous Houses of Yorke and Lancaster, with the death of the good Duke Humphrey: And the banishment and death of the Duke of *Suffolke*, and the Tragicall end of the proud Cardinall of *Winchester*, with the notable Rebellion of *Iacke Cade: And the Duke of Yorkes first claime unto the Crowne.*'   And in the next year appeared another Quarto, from the same publisher, 'The true Tragedie of Richard *Duke of Yorke, and the death of* good King Henrie the Sixt, *with the whole contention betweene* the two Houses Lancaster and Yorke, as it was sundrie times acted by the Right Honourable the Earle of Pembroke his seruants.'   That there is some relation between these two quartos and the second and third parts of *Henry VI* as printed in the Folio is obvious; but what that relation is has been the subject of vigorous and often acrimonious dispute.   One view (which may be called the 'foundation-play' view) is represented by Grant White's theory that 'the First Part of the Contention, The True Tragedy— and, probably, an early form of the First Part of *King Henry the Sixth* unknown to us, were written by Marlowe, Greene, and Shakespeare (and perhaps Peele) together, not improbably as co-labourers for the company known as the Earl of Pembroke's servants, soon after the arrival of Shakespeare in London; and that he, in taking passages, and sometimes whole scenes, from those plays, for his *King Henry the Sixth*, did little more than to reclaim his own.' The other view (which may be called the 'Bad-Quarto' view) was summarised (not without courage, considering the trend of Shake-spearean scholarship of his time) by Halliwell-Phillipps: 'The theory which best agrees with the positive evidences is that which concedes the authorship of the three plays [1. 2. 3. *Henry VI*] to Shakespeare, their production to the year 1592, and the quarto editions of the Second and Third Parts as vamped, imperfect, and blundering versions of the poet's own original dramas.' This view was handled by Furnivall in the best manner of robustious controversy. 'This,' said Furnivall, 'is surely a refuge for the brain-destitute. And if any want-wit can bring what he is pleased to call his mind, to accept for a time this notion of the authorship of *The Contention* and *True Tragedy*, he must be left to grow out of it.' But in 1929 Professor Alexander, in a most able study of the problem,[1] with considerably more urbanity than Furnivall, though with an equal conviction of the destitution of brain in the opposite camp, raised the 'Bad-Quarto' view to something near a certainty. I should hesitate to say that Professor Alexander has proved his point, since he suffers, I think, from a tendency to assume as a premise in his argument the very conclusion which by the argument he is trying to prove,[2] and he does not seem to me wholly convincing (nor indeed himself wholly at ease) in his treatment of certain

---

[1] *Shakespeare's Henry VI and Richard III.*

[2] For example, quite early in the argument we find the statement with regard to the Quarto that 'Warwick's part all through is outstanding for its accuracy.' We have no right to speak of accuracy unless we know in advance that F is the original from which Q was taken. The observable facts are simply that there is a close degree of correspond-ence between the part of Warwick as given in Q and the same part as given in F, from which, taken in isolation, we might just as legitimately argue that F was an 'accurate' reproduction of Q.

minor issues.[1]   But he has at any rate cleared the ground of a deal of lumber of misinterpretation, and set out with great clarity the evidence which the reader can handle for himself, even when he thinks that Professor Alexander's own handling is a trifle over-confident.   To me the evidence is, on the main issue, and at any rate with regard to Part 2, entirely convincing.   There can, I think, be little doubt that *The Contention* is a 'reported text'[2] (using the term in its widest sense) of an original which is represented with at least a high degree of completeness and fidelity by the Folio.   Nor can I see any necessity for assuming either that Shakespeare was rehandling material provided by contemporary dramatists (quite apart from the improbability, well argued by Professor Alexander, of his doing anything of the kind), or that he had a collaborator.   Much of the supposed 'evidence' of parallels is disposed of the moment we accept the theory of a 'reported text,' and for the rest we do well to remember a wise remark of Sir Edmund Chambers, 'I do not think we have adequate criteria for distinguishing with any assurance from the style of his contemporaries that of a young writer still under their influence.'   The second and third parts of

---

[1] For example, the odd coincidence in certain stage-directions between the two texts, a coincidence not too easy to account for, and the assumption of a transcript being by some accident available for a few small portions of Q.   As also the cavalier treatment of Jaggard's reprint of 1619, of which Professor Alexander says, 'That Jaggard had no manuscript at his disposal is a fair inference from the corrections he made.'   If corrections is understood in its narrowest sense this may be true, but there are two remarkable additions in the second scene of *The Contention*, one of a line and a half and one of three lines and a half, both of which correspond (though roughly) to F, and which it is hard to suppose that Jaggard or Jaggard's compositor inserted out of his head.

[2] A 'reported' text in the widest sense need not be one constructed from a shorthand report; it may be one constructed by memorisation, with or without the assistance of one or more of the actors (in this case, according to Alexander, the actor who played Warwick and the actor who doubled Suffolk and Clifford).

the play seem to me here on a different plane from the first part. In the first part I agree with Professor Alexander that it is absurd to suppose that because in a historical play different sections deal with different blocks of historical events there is even a prima facie probability that those different blocks were handled by different writers : but I am also aware of jolts, of a kind of geological 'fault' in the strata, that make it hard for me to suppose that the whole play was written by one writer, unless at very different times. But the personal equation is the poorest sort of evidence, and in any case I think that few readers will be aware of any such 'faults' in the second and third parts. I still regard the Folio as more of an 'edited' text than I think Professor Alexander would be prepared to admit (though I should take the 'editing,' if it occurred, as evidence rather of Heminge and Condell's piety than their dishonesty), and I am prepared therefore to believe that the Folio text has been somewhat 'improved' from its original. And for this reason, and as a matter of interest, I have given a few of the Q versions, whether in the text or the notes.[1] But in the upshot it seems to me clear that the editor of such an edition as this need concern himself and his readers only with the Folio text; and that both he and they can with clear consciences assume that in dealing with that text they are dealing with Shakespeare rather than with a committee.

(I have here given only a conclusion. Any reader who wishes to pursue the topic, which is of the highest interest for the student of the 'determination of Shakespeare's text' but of less interest for the reader of Shakespeare, must be referred to Professor Alexander's study, and also to the Sir Edmund Chambers' *William Shakespeare*,

---

[1] Where a passage in brace brackets { } is followed immediately by one in square brackets, that, in this play, is no more than a method of indicating the extent of the F passage to which the Q parallel is being given.

i. 277-93, who, though accepting the 'reported text' theory in the main, raises some very pertinent problems.

Nor have I entered into the reasons which make me less certain of Professor Alexander's conclusions with regard to Part 3 than with regard to Part 2. To state them at all adequately would require a detailed examination of the available evidence quite beyond the scope of such a preface as this. Very briefly, the *True Tragedy*, as a whole, is much closer to F than *The Contention* is, and there are such long passages where the resemblance amounts so nearly to identity that one begins to think that the reporting—if it was reporting—must have been of uncommon accuracy, and to harbour an uneasy suspicion that for at any rate a good deal of the play there may have been a common MS. original. That is, if the *True Tragedy* stood alone the 'reported text' view would be, I think, less easy to substantiate. But, granted a certain antecedent probability that the text of both Quartos was arrived at by the same means, I think it more than likely that Professor Alexander is right about both.)

Date of Composition. One can only say, on grounds both of general probability and of style, later than Part 1, and not much later.

Source. Again, as for Part 1, Holinshed (Halle) in the first place. There are traces of indebtedness to Fabyan, Grafton, and Stowe. (See Boswell-Stone, *Shakespeare's Holinshed*.)

Duration of Action. For the second part Daniel gives fourteen days with intervals suggesting a period of two years. The historic time is 1445-1455.

Criticism.

Hazlitt.—During the time of the civil wars of York and Lancaster, England was a perfect bear-garden, and Shakespear has given us a very lively picture of the scene. The three parts of *Henry VI* convey a picture of very little else: and are inferior to the other historical plays. They have brilliant passages: but the general groundwork is comparatively poor and meagre, the style 'flat and unraised.'

Dowden.—Among his 'wolfish Earls' Henry is in constant terror, not of being himself torn to pieces, but of their flying at one another's throats. Violent scenes, disturbing the cloistral peace which it would please him to see reign throughout the universe, are hateful and terrible to Henry. He rides out hawking with his Queen and Suffolk, the Cardinal and Gloster; some of the riders hardly able for an hour to conceal their emulation and their hate. Henry takes a languid interest in the sport, but all occasions supply food for his contemplative piety; he suffers from a certain incontinence of devout feeling, and now the falcons set him moralising. A moment after, and the peers, with Margaret among them, are bandying furious words. Henry's anguish is extreme, but he hopes that something may be done by a few moral reflections suitable to the occasion.

KING HENRY VI
SECOND PART

DRAMATIS PERSONÆ

KING HENRY the Sixth.

HUMPHREY, *Duke of Gloucester, his uncle.*

CARDINAL BEAUFORT, *Bishop of Winchester, great-uncle to the King.*

RICHARD PLANTAGENET, *Duke of York.*

EDWARD and RICHARD, *his sons.*

DUKE OF SOMERSET.

DUKE OF SUFFOLK.

DUKE OF BUCKINGHAM.

LORD CLIFFORD.

YOUNG CLIFFORD, *his son.*

EARL OF SALISBURY.

EARL OF WARWICK.

LORD SCALES.

LORD SAY.

SIR HUMPHREY STAFFORD, and WILLIAM STAFFORD, *his brother.*

SIR JOHN STANLEY.

VAUX.

MATTHEW GOFFE.

A Sea-Captain, Master, and Master's-Mate, and WALTER WHITMORE.

Two Gentlemen, *prisoners with Suffolk.*

JOHN HUME and JOHN SOUTHWELL, *priests.*

BOLINGBROKE, *a conjurer.*   ALEXANDER IDEN, *a Kentish gentleman.*

THOMAS HORNER, *an armourer.*   JACK CADE, *a rebel.*

Clerk of Chatham.   PETER, *his man.*

SIMPCOX, *an impostor.*   Mayor of Saint Alban's.

GEORGE BEVIS, JOHN HOLLAND, DICK *the butcher,* SMITH *the weaver,*
  MICHAEL, &c., *followers of Cade.*

Two Murderers.

MARGARET, *Queen to King Henry.*   MARGARET JOURDAIN, *a witch.*

ELEANOR, *Duchess of Gloucester.*   Wife to Simpcox.

Lords, Ladies, and Attendants, Petitioners, Aldermen, a Herald, a
  Beadle, Sheriff, and Officers, Citizens, 'Prentices, Falconers,
  Guards, Soldiers, Messengers, &c.

A Spirit.

SCENE: *England.*

THE SECOND PART OF
KING HENRY VI

Act First

SCENE I

London. The palace

*Flourish of trumpets: then hautboys. Enter, the King,
Humphrey, Duke of Gloucester, Salisbury, Warwick,
and Cardinal Beaufort, on the one side; The Queen,
Suffolk, York, Somerset, and Buckingham, on the other*

Suf. As by your high imperial majesty
I had in charge at my depart for France,
As procurator to your excellence,
To marry Princess Margaret for your grace,
So, in the famous ancient city Tours,
In presence of the Kings of France and Sicil,
The Dukes of Orleans, Calaber, Bretagne and Alençon,
Seven earls, twelve barons, and twenty reverend
　　bishops,
I have perform'd my task and was espous'd,
And humbly now upon my bended knee,　　　　　10

I

In sight of England, and her lordly peers,
Deliver up my title in the queen
To your most gracious hands, that are the substance
Of that great shadow I did represent;
The happiest gift, that ever marquess gave,
The fairest queen, that ever king receiv'd.

King. Suffolk, arise. Welcome, Queen Margaret:
I can express no kinder sign of love
Than this kind kiss. O Lord, that lends me life,
Lend me a heart replete with thankfulness! 20
For Thou hast given me in this beauteous face
A world of earthly blessings to my soul,
If sympathy of love unite our thoughts.

Mar. Great King of England, and my gracious lord,
The mutual conference that my mind hath had,
By day, by night, waking, and in my dreams,
In courtly company, or at my beads,
With you, mine alder-liefest sovereign,
Makes me the bolder to salute my king
With ruder terms, such as my wit affords,
And over-joy of heart doth minister. 30

King. Her sight did ravish, but her grace in speech,
Her words y-clad with wisdom's majesty,
Makes me from wondering fall to weeping joys,
Such is the fulness of my heart's content.

2

Lords, with one cheerful voice, welcome my love.

All. (*kneeling*) Long live Queen Margaret, England's
    happiness !

Mar. We thank you all.   *Flourish*

Suf. My lord protector, so it please your grace,
    Here are the articles of contracted peace   40
    Between our sovereign and the French king Charles,
    For eighteen months concluded by consent.

Glo. (*reads*) 'Imprimis, It is agreed between the French
    king Charles, and William de la Pole Marquess of
    Suffolk, ambassador for Henry King of England,
    that the said Henry shall espouse the Lady Margaret,
    daughter unto Reignier King of Naples, Sicilia, and
    Jerusalem, and crown her Queen of England, ere
    the thirtieth of May next ensuing. Item, that the
    duchy of Anjou, and the county of Maine, shall be   50
    released and delivered to the king her father—'
                                        [*Lets the paper fall*]

King. Uncle, how now ?

Glo.   Pardon me, gracious lord,
    Some sudden qualm hath struck me at the heart,
    And dimm'd mine eyes, that I can read no further.

King. Uncle of Winchester, I pray read on.

Car. (*reads*) 'Item, It is further agreed between them,
    that the duchies of Anjou and Maine shall be released

b 38   3

and delivered over to the king her father, and she
sent over of the King of England's own proper cost
and charges, without having any dowry.'   60

*King.*They please us well.   Lord marquess, kneel down:
We here create thee the first duke of Suffolk,
And gird thee with the sword.   Cousin of York,
We here discharge your grace from being regent
I' the parts of France, till term of eighteen months
Be full expir'd.   Thanks, uncle Winchester,
Gloucester, York, Buckingham, Somerset,
Salisbury, and Warwick;
We thank you all for this great favour done,
In entertainment to my princely queen.   70
Come, let us in, and with all speed provide
To see her coronation be perform'd.

Exeunt King, Queen, and Suffolk, [and Duke
Humphrey stays all the rest]

Glo. Brave peers of England, pillars of the state,
To you Duke Humphrey must unload his grief,
Your grief, the common grief of all the land.
What? did my brother Henry spend his youth,
His valour, coin, and people, in the wars?
Did he so often lodge in open field,
In winter's cold, and summer's parching heat,
To conquer France, his true inheritance?   80

4

And did my brother Bedford toil his wits,
To keep by policy what Henry got:
Have you yourselves, Somerset, Buckingham,
Brave York, Salisbury, and victorious Warwick,
Receiv'd deep scars in France and Normandy:
Or hath mine uncle Beaufort, and myself,
With all the learned council of the realm,
Studied so long, sat in the council-house
Early and late, debating to and fro
How France and Frenchmen might be kept in awe,   90
And had his highness in his infancy
Crowned in Paris in despite of foes:
And shall these labours and these honours die?
Shall Henry's conquest, Bedford's vigilance,
Your deeds of war, and all our counsel die?
O peers of England, shameful is this league,
Fatal this marriage, cancelling your fame,
Blotting your names from books of memory,
Razing the characters of your renown,
Defacing monuments of conquer'd France,   100
Undoing all as all had never been!

Car. Nephew, what means this passionate discourse,
This peroration with such circumstance?
For France, 'tis ours; and we will keep it still.

Glo. Ay, uncle, we will keep it, if we can;

5

But now it is impossible we should :
Suffolk, the new-made duke that rules the roast,
Hath given the duchy of Anjou and Maine
Unto the poor King Reignier, whose large style
Agrees not with the leanness of his purse. 110

Sal. Now, by the death of Him that died for all,
These counties were the keys of Normandy.
But wherefore weeps Warwick, my valiant son ?

War. For grief that they are past recovery :
For were there hope to conquer them again,
My sword should shed hot blood, mine eyes no tears.
Anjou and Maine ? myself did win them both ;
Those provinces these arms of mine did conquer,
And are the cities, that I got with wounds,
Deliver'd up again with peaceful words ? 120
Mort Dieu !

Yo. For Suffolk's duke, may he be suffocate,
That dims the honour of this warlike isle !
France should have torn and rent my very heart,
Before I would have yielded to this league.
I never read but England's kings have had
Large sums of gold and dowries with their wives,
And our King Henry gives away his own,
To match with her that brings no vantages.

Glo. A proper jest, and never heard before, 130

6

That Suffolk should demand a whole fifteenth,
For costs and charges in transporting her!
She should have stay'd in France, and starv'd in
    France,
Before—

Car. My Lord of Gloucester, now ye grow too hot;
    It was the pleasure of my lord the king.

Glo. My lord of Winchester, I know your mind;
    'Tis not my speeches that you do mislike;
    But 'tis my presence that doth trouble ye.
    Rancour will out; proud prelate, in thy face   **140**
    I see thy fury: if I longer stay,
    We shall begin our ancient bickerings.
    Lordings, farewell; and say, when I am gone,
    I prophesied France will be lost ere long.   *Exit*

Car. So, there goes our protector in a rage.
    'Tis known to you he is mine enemy,
    Nay, more, an enemy unto you all,
    And no great friend, I fear me, to the king.
    Consider, lords, he is the next of blood,
    And heir apparent to the English crown: **150**
    Had Henry got an empire by his marriage,
    And all the wealthy kingdoms of the west,
    There's reason he should be displeas'd at it.
    Look to it, lords; let not his smoothing words

Bewitch your hearts ; be wise and circumspect.
What though the common people favour him,
Calling him ' Humphrey, the good Duke of Gloucester,'
Clapping their hands, and crying with loud voice,
' Jesu maintain your royal excellence ! '
With ' God preserve the good Duke Humphrey ! ' 160
I fear me, lords, for all this flattering gloss,
He will be found a dangerous protector.

Buc. Why should he then protect our sovereign,
He being of age to govern of himself ?
Cousin of Somerset, join you with me,
And all together, with the Duke of Suffolk,
We 'll quickly hoise Duke Humphrey from his seat.

Car. This weighty business will not brook delay,
I 'll to the Duke of Suffolk presently.   *Exit*

Som. Cousin of Buckingham, though Humphrey's pride 170
And greatness of his place be grief to us,
Yet let us watch the haughty cardinal :
His insolence is more intolerable
Than all the princes in the land beside :
If Gloucester be displac'd, he 'll be protector.

Buc. Or thou or I, Somerset, will be protector.
Despite Duke Humphrey, or the cardinal.

        Exeunt Buckingham and Somerset

Sal. Pride went before, ambition follows him.

While these do labour for their own preferment,
Behoves it us to labour for the realm.   180
I never saw but Humphrey Duke of Gloucester
Did bear him like a noble gentleman.
Oft have I seen the haughty cardinal,
More like a soldier than a man o' the church,
As stout and proud as he were lord of all,
Swear like a ruffian, and demean himself
Unlike the ruler of a commonweal.
Warwick, my son, the comfort of my age,
Thy deeds, thy plainness, and thy housekeeping,
Hath won the greatest favour of the commons,   190
Excepting none but good Duke Humphrey:
And, brother York, thy acts in Ireland,
In bringing them to civil discipline,
Thy late exploits done in the heart of France,
When thou wert regent for our sovereign,
Have made thee fear'd and honour'd of the people;
Join we together for the public good,
In what we can, to bridle and suppress
The pride of Suffolk and the cardinal,
With Somerset's and Buckingham's ambition;   200
And, as we may, cherish Duke Humphrey's deeds,
While they do tend the profit of the land.

War. So God help Warwick, as he loves the land,

And common profit of his country!

Yo. (*aside*) And so says York, for he hath greatest cause.

Sal. Then let's make haste away, and look unto the main.

War. Unto the main! O father, Maine is lost:
That Maine which by main force Warwick did win,
And would have kept, so long as breath did last!
Main chance, father, you meant; but I meant Maine,   210
Which I will win from France, or else be slain.

> *Exeunt Warwick and Salisbury*

Yo. Anjou and Maine are given to the French,
Paris is lost, the state of Normandy
Stands on a tickle point, now they are gone:
Suffolk concluded on the articles,
The peers agreed, and Henry was well pleas'd,
To change two dukedoms for a duke's fair dauaghter.
I cannot blame them all: what is 't to them?
'Tis thine they give away, and not their own.
Pirates may make cheap pennyworths of their pillage,
And purchase friends, and give to courtezans,   221
Still revelling like lords till all be gone;
While as the silly owner of the goods
Weeps over them, and wrings his hapless hands,
And shakes his head, and trembling stands aloof,
While all is shar'd, and all is borne away,
Ready to starve, and dare not touch his own:

So York must sit, and fret, and bite his tongue,
While his own lands are bargain'd for and sold.
Methinks the realms of England, France, and Ireland 230
Bear that proportion to my flesh and blood
As did the fatal brand Althæa burn'd   †
Unto the prince's heart of Calydon.
Anjou and Maine both given unto the French ?
Cold news for me ; for I had hope of France,
Even as I have of fertile England's soil.
A day will come when York shall claim his own,
And therefore I will take the Nevils' parts,
And make a show of love to proud Duke Humphrey,
And when I spy advantage, claim the crown,   240
For that 's the golden mark I seek to hit :
Nor shall proud Lancaster usurp my right,
Nor hold the sceptre in his childish fist,
Nor wear the diadem upon his head,
Whose church-like humours fits not for a crown.
Then, York, be still awhile, till time do serve :
Watch thou, and wake when others be asleep,
To pry into the secrets of the state,
Till Henry, surfeiting in joys of love,
With his new bride and England's dear-bought queen,
And Humphrey with the peers be fall'n at jars :   251
Then will I raise aloft the milk-white rose,

With whose sweet smell the air shall be perfum'd,
And in my standard bear the arms of York,
To grapple with the house of Lancaster,
And, force perforce, I'll make him yield the crown,
Whose bookish rule hath pull'd fair England down.

Exit

SCENE II

The Duke of Gloucester's house

Enter Duke Humphrey and his wife Eleanor

Ele. Why droops my lord like over-ripen'd corn,
Hanging the head at Ceres' plenteous load?
Why doth the great Duke Humphrey knit his brows,
As frowning at the favours of the world?
Why are thine eyes fix'd to the sullen earth,
Gazing on that which seems to dim thy sight?
What seest thou there? King Henry's diadem,
Enchas'd with all the honours of the world?
If so, gaze on, and grovel on thy face,
Until thy head be circled with the same.
Put forth thy hand, reach at the glorious gold.
What, is't too short? I'll lengthen it with mine;
And, having both together heav'd it up,
We'll both together lift our heads to heaven,

10

And never more abase our sight so low
As to vouchsafe one glance unto the ground.

Glo. O Nell, sweet Nell, if thou dost love thy lord,
Banish the canker of ambitious thoughts.
And may that thought, when I imagine ill
Against my king and nephew, virtuous Henry,   20
Be my last breathing in this mortal world!
My troublous dreams this night doth make me sad.

Ele. What dream'd my lord? tell me, and I'll requite it
With sweet rehearsal of my morning's dream.

Glo. Methought this staff, mine office-badge in court,   †
Was broke in twain; by whom, I have forgot,
But, as I think, it was by the cardinal;
And on the pieces of the broken wand
Were plac'd the heads of Edmund Duke of Somerset,
And William de la Pole, first Duke of Suffolk.   30
This was my dream: what it doth bode, God knows.

Ele. Tut, this was nothing but an argument,
That he that breaks a stick of Gloucester's grove
Shall lose his head for his presumption.
But list to me, my Humphrey, my sweet duke:
Methought, I sat in seat of majesty,
In the cathedral church of Westminster,
And in that chair where kings and queens are crown'd;
Where Henry and dame Margaret kneel'd to me,

13

And on my head did set the diadem. 40

Glo. Nay, Eleanor, then must I chide outright :
Presumptuous dame, ill-nurtur'd Eleanor,
Art thou not second woman in the realm ?
And the protector's wife, belov'd of him ?
Hast thou not worldly pleasure at command,
Above the reach or compass of thy thought ?
And wilt thou still be hammering treachery,
To tumble down thy husband, and thyself,
From top of honour, to disgrace's feet ?
Away from me, and let me hear no more ! 50

Ele. What, what, my lord ? are you so choleric
With Eleanor, for telling but her dream ?
Next time I'll keep my dreams unto myself,
And not be check'd.

Glo. Nay, be not angry, I am pleas'd again.

Enter Messenger

Mes. My lord protector, 'tis his highness' pleasure
You do prepare to ride unto Saint Alban's,
Whereas the king and queen do mean to hawk.

Glo. I go.   Come, Nell, thou wilt ride with us ?

Ele. Yes, my good lord, I'll follow presently. 60

Exeunt Gloucester and Messenger

Follow I must, I cannot go before, †
While Gloucester bears this base and humble mind.

14

Were I a man, a duke, and next of blood,
I would remove these tedious stumbling-blocks,
And smooth my way upon their headless necks ;
And, being a woman, I will not be slack
To play my part in Fortune's pageant.
Where are you there ? Sir John ! nay, fear not, man,
We are alone, here's none but thee and I.

Enter Hume

Hu. Jesus preserve your royal majesty !   70

Ele. What say'st thou ? majesty ! I am but grace.

Hu. But, by the grace of God, and Hume's advice,
   Your grace's title shall be multiplied.

Ele. What say'st thou, man ? hast thou as yet conferr'd
   With Margery Jourdain, the cunning witch,
   With Roger Bolingbroke, the conjurer ?
   And will they undertake to do me good ?

Hu. This they have promised, to show your highness
   A spirit rais'd from depth of under-ground,
   That shall make answer to such questions   80
   As by your grace shall be propounded him.

Ele. {It is enough, I 'll think upon the questions :   †
   When from Saint Alban's we do make return,
   We 'll see these things effected to the full.
   Here, Hume, take this reward ; make merry, man,
   With thy confederates in this weighty cause.} *Exit*

15

[Thanks, good Sir John : some two days hence, I guess,
Will fit our time ; then see that they be here ;
For now the king is riding to St Alban's,
And all the dukes and earls along with him :
When they be gone, then safely they may come,
And on the backside of my orchard here
There cast their spells in silence of the night,
And so resolve us of the thing we wish,
Till when, drink that for my sake ; and so farewell.]

Hu. Hume must make merry with the duchess' gold ;
Marry, and shall.   But, how now, Sir John Hume ?
Seal up your lips, and give no words but mum :
The business asketh silent secrecy.   90
Dame Eleanor gives gold, to bring the witch :
Gold cannot come amiss, were she a devil.
Yet have I gold flies from another coast ;
I dare not say, from the rich cardinal,
And from the great and new-made Duke of Suffolk ;
Yet I do find it so ; for, to be plain,
They (knowing Dame Eleanor's aspiring humour)
Have hired me to undermine the duchess,
And buz these conjurations in her brain.
They say ' A crafty knave does need no broker ;'   100
Yet am I Suffolk and the cardinal's broker.
Hume, if you take not heed, you shall go near

To call them both a pair of crafty knaves.
Well, so it stands ; and thus, I fear, at last
Hume's knavery will be the duchess' wreck,
And her attainture will be Humphrey's fall :
Sort how it will, I shall have gold for all.   *Exit*

SCENE III

The palace

*Enter three or four Petitioners, Peter, the Armourer's
man, being one*

1.P. My masters, let's stand close : my lord protector
     will come this way by and by, and then we may
     deliver our supplications in the quill.

2.P. Marry, the Lord protect him, for he's a good man,
     Jesu bless him !

Enter Suffolk and Queen

Pet. Here a' comes, methinks, and the queen with him.
     I'll be the first, sure.

2.P. Come back, fool, this is the Duke of Suffolk, and
     not my lord protector.

Suf. How now, fellow ? wouldst any thing with me ?   10

1.P. I pray, my lord, pardon me, I took ye for my lord
     protector.

Mar. (*reading*) 'To my Lord Protector?' Are your supplications to his lordship? Let me see them: what is thine?

1.P. Mine is, an't please your grace, against John Goodman, my lord cardinal's man, for keeping my house, and lands, and wife and all, from me.

Suf. Thy wife too? that's some wrong, indeed. What's yours? What's here? (*reads*) 'Against the Duke of Suffolk, for enclosing the commons of Melford.' How now, sir knave?

2.P. Alas, sir, I am but a poor petitioner of our whole township.

Pet. (*giving his petition*) Against my master, Thomas Horner, for saying that the Duke of York was rightful heir to the crown.

Mar. What say'st thou? did the Duke of York say he was rightful heir to the crown?

Pet. That my master was? no, forsooth: my master said that he was, and that the king was an usurper.

Suf. Who is there? (*enter Servant.*) Take this fellow in, and send for his master with a pursuivant presently: we'll hear more of your matter before the king.

> *Exit Servant with Peter*

Mar. And as for you, that love to be protected
Under the wings of our protector's grace,

Begin your suits anew, and sue to him.

Tears the supplications

Away, base cullions !   Suffolk, let them go.

All. Come, let 's be gone.   *Exeunt*

*Mar.*My Lord of Suffolk, say, is this the guise,   40
    Is this the fashions in the court of England ?
    Is this the government of Britain's isle ?
    And this the royalty of Albion's king ?
    What, shall King Henry be a pupil still,
    Under the surly Gloucester's governance ?
    Am I a queen in title and in style,
    And must be made a subject to a duke ?
    I tell thee, Pole, when in the city Tours
    Thou ran'st a tilt in honour of my love,
    And stol'st away the ladies' hearts of France,   50
    I thought King Henry had resembled thee,
    In courage, courtship and proportion :
    But all his mind is bent to holiness,
    To number Ave-Maries on his beads ;
    His champions are the prophets and apostles,
    His weapons holy saws of sacred writ,
    His study is his tilt-yard, and his loves
    Are brazen images of canonized saints.
    I would the college of the cardinals
    Would choose him pope, and carry him to Rome,   60

And set the triple crown upon his head :
That were a state fit for his holiness.

Suf. Madam, be patient : as I was cause
Your highness came to England, so will I
In England work your grace's full content.

*Mar.*Beside the haughty protector, have we Beaufort,
The imperious churchman, Somerset, Buckingham,
And grumbling York ; and not the least of these
But can do more in England than the king.

Suf. And he of these that can do most of all   70
Cannot do more in England than the Nevils :
Salisbury and Warwick are no simple peers.

*Mar.*Not all these lords do vex me half so much
As that proud dame, the lord protector's wife.
She sweeps it through the court with troops of ladies,
More like an empress than Duke Humphrey's wife :
Strangers in court do take her for the queen :
She bears a duke's revenues on her back,
And in her heart she scorns our poverty :
Shall I not live to be aveng'd on her ?   80
Contemptuous base-born callet as she is,
She vaunted 'mongst her minions t' other day,
The very train of her worst wearing gown
Was better worth than all my father's lands,
Till Suffolk gave two dukedoms for his daughter.

Suf. Madam, myself have lim'd a bush for her,
And plac'd a quire of such enticing birds,
That she will light to listen to the lays,
And never mount to trouble you again.
So let her rest : and, madam, list to me ;   90
For I am bold to counsel you in this ;
Although we fancy not the cardinal,
Yet must we join with him and with the lords,
Till we have brought Duke Humphrey in disgrace.
As for the Duke of York, this late complaint
Will make but little for his benefit.
So, one by one, we 'll weed them all at last,
And you yourself shall steer the happy helm.

Sound a Sennet.   Enter the King, Duke Humphrey of Gloucester,
Cardinal Beaufort, Buckingham, York, Somerset, Salis-
bury, Warwick, and the Duchess of Gloucester

King. For my part, noble lords, I care not which,
Or Somerset, or York, all 's one to me.   100

Yo. If York have ill demean'd himself in France,
Then let him be denay'd the regentship.

Som. If Somerset be unworthy of the place,
Let York be regent, I will yield to him.

War. Whether your grace be worthy, yea or no,
Dispute not that : York is the worthier.

Car. Ambitious Warwick, let thy betters speak.

War. The cardinal's not my better in the field.

Buc. All in this presence are thy betters, Warwick.

War. Warwick may live to be the best of all. 110

Sal. Peace, son! and show some reason, Buckingham,
 Why Somerset should be preferr'd in this.

Mar. Because the king, forsooth, will have it so.

{*Glo.* Madam, the king is old enough himself †
 To give his censure : these are no women's matters.

Mar. If he be old enough, what needs your grace
 To be protector of his excellence ?}

[*Glo.* Madam, our king is old enough himself
 To give his answer without your consent.

Mar. If he be old enough, what needs your grace
 To be protector over him so long ?]

Glo. Madam, I am protector of the realm,
 And at his pleasure will resign my place.

Suf. Resign it then and leave thine insolence. 120
 Since thou wert king—as who is king but thou ?—
 The commonwealth hath daily run to wreck,
 The Dauphin hath prevail'd beyond the seas,
 And all the peers and nobles of the realm
 Have been as bondmen to thy sovereignty.

Car. The commons hast thou rack'd, the clergy's bags
 Are lank and lean with thy extortions.

Som. Thy sumptuous buildings, and thy wife's attire,

  Have cost a mass of public treasury.

Buc. Thy cruelty in execution   130

  Upon offenders hath exceeded law,

  And left thee to the mercy of the law.

Mar. Thy sale of offices and towns in France,

  If they were known, as the suspect is great,

  Would make thee quickly hop without thy head.

     Exit Gloucester.   The Queen drops her fan

  Give me my fan : what, minion, can ye not ?

      She gives the Duchess a box on the ear

  I cry you mercy, madam ; was it you ?

Ele. Was 't I ? yea, I it was, proud Frenchwoman :

  Could I come near your beauty with my nails,

  I could set my ten commandments in your face. 140

King. Sweet aunt, be quiet, 'twas against her will.

Ele. Against her will, good king ? look to 't in time,

  She 'll hamper thee, and dandle thee like a baby :

  Though in this place most master wear no breeches, †

  She shall not strike Dame Eleanor unreveng'd. *Exit*

Buc. Lord cardinal, I will follow Eleanor,

  And listen after Humphrey, how he proceeds :

  She 's tickled now ; her fume needs no spurs, †

  She 'll gallop far enough to her destruction. *Exit*

     Re-enter Gloucester

Glo. Now, lords, my choler being over-blown   150

23

With walking once about the quadrangle,
I come to talk of commonwealth affairs.
As for your spiteful false objections,
Prove them, and I lie open to the law:
But God in mercy so deal with my soul,
As I in duty love my king and country!
But, to the matter that we have in hand:
I say, my sovereign, York is meetest man
To be your regent in the realm of France.

Suf. Before we make election, give me leave   160
To show some reason, of no little force,
That York is most unmeet of any man.

Yo. I'll tell thee, Suffolk, why I am unmeet:
First, for I cannot flatter thee in pride;
Next, if I be appointed for the place,
My Lord of Somerset will keep me here,
Without discharge, money, or furniture,
Till France be won into the Dauphin's hands:
Last time I danc'd attendance on his will
Till Paris was besieg'd, famish'd, and lost.   170

War. That can I witness, and a fouler fact
Did never traitor in the land commit.

Suf. Peace, headstrong Warwick!

War. Image of pride, why should I hold my peace?

Enter Horner, the Armourer, and his man Peter, guarded

Suf. Because here is a man accus'd of treason :
　　Pray God the Duke of York excuse himself !

Yo. Doth any one accuse York for a traitor ?

King. What mean'st thou, Suffolk ? tell me, what are these ?

Suf. Please it your majesty, this is the man
　　That doth accuse his master of high treason :　　180
　　His words were these : that Richard, Duke of York,
　　Was rightful heir unto the English crown,
　　And that your majesty was an usurper.

King. Say, man, were these thy words ?

Hor. An 't shall please your majesty, I never said nor
　　thought any such matter : God is my witness, I am
　　falsely accus'd by the villain.

Pet. By these ten bones, my lords, he did speak them to
　　me in the garret one night, as we were scouring my
　　Lord of York's armour.　　190

Yo. Base dunghill villain and mechanical,
　　I'll have thy head for this thy traitor's speech.
　　I do beseech your royal majesty,
　　Let him have all the rigour of the law.

Hor. Alas, my lord, hang me, if ever I spake the words.
　　My accuser is my 'prentice, and when I did correct
　　him for his fault the other day, he did vow upon
　　his knees he would be even with me : I have good

witness of this ; therefore I beseech your majesty,
do not cast away an honest man for a villain's **200**
accusation.

King. Uncle, what shall we say to this in law ?

Glo. This doom, my lord, if I may judge :
Let Somerset be regent o'er the French,
Because in York this breeds suspicion :
And let these have a day appointed them
For single combat, in convenient place,
For he hath witness of his servant's malice :
This is the law, and this Duke Humphrey's doom.

Som. I humbly thank your royal majesty. **210**

Hor. And I accept the combat willingly.

Pet. Alas, my lord, I cannot fight ; for God's sake, pity
my case. The spite of man prevaileth against me.
O Lord, have mercy upon me ! I shall never be able
to fight a blow. O Lord, my heart !

Glo. Sirrah, or you must fight, or else be hang'd.

King. Away with them to prison ; and the day of combat
shall be the last of the next month. Come, Somerset,
we'll see thee sent away. *Flourish. Exeunt*

SCENE IV

Gloucester's garden

*Enter Margery Jourdain, Hume, Southwell.
and Bolingbroke*

Hu. Come, my masters ; the duchess, I tell you, expects
performance of your promises.

Bol. Master Hume, we are therefore provided : will her
ladyship behold and hear our exorcisms ?

Hu. Ay, what else ? fear you not her courage.

Bol. I have heard her reported to be a woman of an in-
vincible spirit : but it shall be convenient, Master
Hume, that you be by her aloft, while we be busy
below ; and so, I pray you, go in God's name, and
leave us. (*exit Hume.*) Mother Jourdain, be you   10
prostrate, and grovel on the earth ; John Southwell,
read you, and let us to our work.

Enter Duchess aloft, Hume following

Ele. Well said, my masters, and welcome all.
To this gear, the sooner the better.

Bol. Patience, good lady, wizards know their times :
Deep night, dark night, the silent of the night,
The time of night when Troy was set on fire,
The time when screech-owls cry, and ban-dogs howl,

27

And spirits walk, and ghosts break up their graves ;
That time best fits the work we have in hand.   20
Madam, sit you, and fear not : whom we raise,
We will make fast within a hallow'd verge.

> *Here they do the ceremonies belonging, and make
> the circle ; Bolingbroke or Southwell reads,
> Conjuro te, &c.   It thunders and lightens
> terribly ; then the Spirit riseth.*

Spi. Adsum.

Jou. Asmath,
By the eternal God, whose name and power
Thou tremblest at, answer that I shall ask ;
For till thou speak, thou shalt not pass from hence.

Spi. Ask what thou wilt.   That I had said and done !

Bol. ' First of the king : what shall of him become ? '

> *Reading out of a paper*

Spi. The duke yet lives that Henry shall depose ;   30
But him outlive, and die a violent death.

> *As the Spirit speaks, Southwell writes the answer*

Bol. ' What fates await the Duke of Suffolk ? '

Spi. By water shall he die, and take his end.

Bol. ' What shall befall the Duke of Somerset ? '

Spi. Let him shun castles ;
Safer shall he be upon the sandy plains
Than where castles mounted stand.

Have done, for more I hardly can endure.

Bol. {Descend to darkness and the burning lake !   †
False fiend, avoid !   40

> *Thunder and lightning.   Exit Spirit*}

[Then down, I say, unto the damned pole,
Where Pluto in his fiery wagon sits,
Riding amidst the sing'd and parched smokes
The road of Dytas by the river Styx ;
There howl and burn for ever in those flames.
Rise, Jourdain, rise, and stay thy charming spells :
Sons, we are betray'd.]

> *Enter the Duke of York and the Duke of Buckingham*
> *with their Guard and break in*

Yo. Lay hands upon these traitors and their trash.
Beldam, I think we watch'd you at an inch.
What, madam, are you there ? the king and common-
         weal
Are deeply indebted for this piece of pains ;
My lord protector will, I doubt it not,
See you well guerdon'd for these good deserts.

Ele. Not half so bad as thine to England's king,
Injurious duke, that threatest where 's no cause.

Buc. True, madam, none at all : what call you this ?
Away with them, let them be clapp'd up close,   50
And kept asunder.   You, madam, shall with us.

Stafford, take her to thee.

Exeunt above Duchess and Hume, guarded

We 'll see your trinkets here all forthcoming.
All, away !

Exeunt Guard with Jourdain, Southwell, &c.

Yo. Lord Buckingham, methinks you watch'd her well :
A pretty plot, well chosen to build upon !
Now, pray, my lord, let's see the devil's writ.
What have we here ?   *Reads*
' The duke yet lives, that Henry shall depose ;
But him outlive, and die a violent death.'   60
Why this is just
' Aio te, Æacida, Romanos vincere posse.'   †
Well, to the rest :
' Tell me, what fate awaits the Duke of Suffolk ?
By water shall he die, and take his end.
What shall betide the Duke of Somerset ?
Let him shun castles ;
Safer shall he be upon the sandy plains
Than where castles mounted stand.'
Come, come, my lords ;   70
These oracles are hardly attain'd,
And hardly understood.
The king is now in progress towards Saint Alban's,
With him the husband of this lovely lady :

Thither go these news, as fast as horse can carry them :
A sorry breakfast for my lord protector.

Buc Your grace shall give me leave, my Lord of York,
To be the post, in hope of his reward.

Yo. At your pleasure, my good lord.   Who 's within
there, ho !

Enter a Serving-man

Invite my Lords of Salisbury and Warwick   80
To sup with me to-morrow night.   Away !   *Exeunt*

Act Second

SCENE I

Saint Alban's

Enter the King, Queen, Gloucester, Cardinal, and Suffolk,
with Falconers halloing

Mar. Believe me, lords, for flying at the brook,
I saw not better sport these seven years' day :
Yea, by your leave, the wind was very high,
And, ten to one, old Joan had not gone out.

King. But what a point, my lord, your falcon made,
And what a pitch she flew above the rest !

To see how God in all His creatures works !
Yea, man and birds are fain of climbing high.

Suf. No marvel, an it like your majesty,
My lord protector's hawks do tower so well ;   10
They know their master loves to be aloft,
And bears his thoughts above his falcon's pitch.

Glo. My lord, 'tis but a base ignoble mind
That mounts no higher than a bird can soar.

Car. I thought as much ; he would be above the clouds.

Glo. Ay, my lord cardinal ? how think you by that ?
Were it not good your grace could fly to heaven ?

King. The treasury of everlasting joy.

Car. Thy heaven is on earth, thine eyes and thoughts
Beat on a crown, the treasure of thy heart ;   20
Pernicious protector, dangerous peer,
That smooth'st it so with king and commonweal.

Glo. What, cardinal, is your priesthood grown peremptory ?
Tantæne animis cælestibus iræ ?
Churchmen so hot ? good uncle, hide such malice ;
With such holiness can you do it ?

Suf. No malice, sir, no more than well becomes
So good a quarrel and so bad a peer.

Glo. As who, my lord ?

Suf.   Why, as you, my lord,
An 't like your lordly lord-protectorship.   30

Glo. Why, Suffolk, England knows thine insolence.

Mar. And thy ambition, Gloucester.

King. I prithee, peace, good queen,
        And whet not on these furious peers ;
        For blessed are the peacemakers on earth.

Car. Let me be blessed for the peace I make
        Against this proud protector with my sword !

Glo. *(aside to Car.)* Faith, holy uncle, would 'twere come
        to that !

Car. *(aside to Glo.)* Marry, when thou dar'st.

Glo. *(aside to Car.)* Make up no factious numbers for the
        matter ;   40
        In thine own person answer thy abuse.

Car. *(aside to Glo.)* Ay, where thou dar'st not peep : an
        if thou dar'st,
        This evening, on the east side of the grove.

King. How now, my lords ?

Car.   Believe me, cousin Gloucester,
        Had not your man put up the fowl so suddenly,
        We had had more sport.   *(aside to Glo.)* Come with
        thy two-hand sword.

Glo. True, uncle.

Car. *(aside to Glo.)* Are ye advis'd ? the east side of the
        grove.

Glo. *(aside to Car.)* Cardinal, I am with you.

King.   Why, how now, uncle Gloucester?

Glo. Talking of hawking; nothing else, my lord.   50

     (*aside to Car.*) Now, by God's mother, priest, I 'll

        shave your crown for this,

     Or all my fence shall fail.

Car. (*aside to Glo.*) Medice, teipsum—

     Protector, see to 't well, protect yourself.

King. The winds grow high, so do your stomachs, lords:

     How irksome is this music to my heart!

     When such strings jar, what hope of harmony?

     I pray, my lords, let me compound this strife.

     Enter a Townsman of Saint Alban's, crying ' A miracle !'

Glo. What means this noise?

     Fellow, what miracle dost thou proclaim?   60

Towns. A miracle! a miracle!

Suf. Come to the king, and tell him what miracle.

Towns. Forsooth, a blind man at Saint Alban's shrine,

     Within this half-hour hath receiv'd his sight,

     A man that ne'er saw in his life before.

King. Now, God be prais'd, that to believing souls

     Gives light in darkness, comfort in despair!

     Enter the Mayor of Saint Alban's and his brethren, bearing

     Simpcox, between two in a chair, Simpcox's Wife following

Car. Here comes the townsmen, on procession,

     To present your highness with the man.

*King.*Great is his comfort in this earthly vale,   70
    Although by his sight his sin be multiplied.

Glo. Stand by, my masters, bring him near the king ;
    His highness' pleasure is to talk with him.

*King.*Good fellow, tell us here the circumstance,
    That we for thee may glorify the Lord.
    What, hast thou been long blind and now restor'd ?

Sim. Born blind, an 't please your grace.

*Wife.*Ay, indeed, was he.

Suf. What woman is this ?

*Wife.*His wife, an 't like your worship.   80

Glo. Hadst thou been his mother, thou couldst have better
    told.

*King.*Where wert thou born ?

Sim. At Berwick in the north, an 't like your grace.

*King.*Poor soul, God's goodness hath been great to thee :
    Let never day nor night unhallow'd pass,
    But still remember what the Lord hath done.

*Mar.*Tell me, good fellow, cam'st thou here by chance,
    Or of devotion, to this holy shrine ?

Sim. God knows, of pure devotion, being call'd
    A hundred times and oftener, in my sleep,   90
    By good Saint Alban ; who said, ' Simpcox, come,
    Come, offer at my shrine, and I will help thee.'

*Wife.*Most true, forsooth ; and many time and oft

Myself have heard a voice to call him so.

Car. What, art thou lame ?

Sim. Ay, God Almighty help me !

Suf. How cam'st thou so ?

Sim. A fall off of a tree.

Wife. A plum-tree, master.

Glo. How long hast thou been blind ?

Sim. O, born so, master.

Glo. What, and wouldst climb a tree ?

Sim. But that in all my life, when I was a youth.

Wife. Too true, and bought his climbing very dear.   100

Glo. Mass, thou lov'st plums well, that wouldst venture so.

Sim. Alas, good master, my wife desir'd some damsons,
    And made me climb, with danger of my life.

Glo. A subtle knave ! but yet it shall not serve.
    Let me see thine eyes : wink now, now open them :
    In my opinion yet thou see'st not well.

Sim. Yes, master, clear as day, I thank God and Saint
        Alban.

Glo. Say'st thou me so ?   What colour is this cloak of ?

Sim. Red, master, red as blood.   †

[*Glo.* And his cloak ?

Sim. Why, that 's green.

Glo. And what colour 's his hose ?

Sim. Yellow, master, yellow as gold.]

36

Glo. Why, that's well said.   What colour is my gown 110
   of ?

Sim. Black, forsooth, coal-black as jet.

King. Why, then, thou kno'wst what colour jet is of ?

Suf. And yet, I think, jet did he never see.

Glo. But cloaks and gowns, before this day, a many.

Wife. Never before this day, in all his life.

Glo. Tell me, sirrah, what's my name ?

Sim. Alas, master, I know not.

Glo. What's his name ?

Sim. I know not.

Glo. Nor his ? 120

Sim. No, indeed, master.

Glo. What's thine own name ?

Sim. Saunder Simpcox, an if it please you, master.

Glo. Then, Saunder, sit there, the lying'st knave in
   Christendom.   If thou hadst been born blind,
   thou mightst as well have known all our names as
   thus to name the several colours we do wear.   Sight
   may distinguish of colours, but suddenly to nominate
   them all, it is impossible.   My lords, Saint Alban
   here hath done a miracle ; and would ye not think 130
   his cunning to be great, that could restore this
   cripple to his legs again ?

Sim. O master, that you could !

Glo. My masters of Saint Alban's, have you not beadles
   in your town, and things called whips ?

May. Yes, my lord, if it please your grace.

Glo. Then send for one presently.

May. Sirrah, go fetch the beadle hither straight.

Exit an Attendant

Glo. Now fetch me a stool hither by and by. Now,   140
   sirrah, if you mean to save yourself from whipping,
   leap me over this stool and run away.

Sim. Alas, master, I am not able to stand alone :
   You go about to torture me in vain.

Enter a Beadle with whips

Glo. Well, sir, we must have you find your legs. Sirrah
   beadle, whip him till he leap over that same stool.

Bead. I will, my lord. Come on, sirrah, off with your
   doublet quickly.

Sim. Alas, master, what shall I do ? I am not able to
   stand.

*After the Beadle hath hit him {once} [one girke]
      he leaps over the stool and runs away ; and
      they follow and cry, ' A miracle ! '*

King. O God, seest Thou this, and bearest so long ?   150

Mar. It made me laugh to see the villain run.

Glo. Follow the knave, and take this drab away.

Wife. Alas, sir, we did it for pure need.

Glo. Let them be whipp'd through every market-town,
  till they come to Berwick, from whence they came.

Exeunt Wife, Beadle, Mayor, &c.

Car. Duke Humphrey has done a miracle to-day.

Suf. True ; made the lame to leap and fly away.

Glo. But you have done more miracles than I ;
  You made in a day, my lord, whole towns to fly.

Enter Buckingham

King. What tidings with our cousin Buckingham ?   160

Buc. Such as my heart doth tremble to unfold.
  A sort of naughty persons, lewdly bent,
  Under the countenance and confederacy
  Of Lady Eleanor, the protector's wife,
  The ringleader and head of all this rout,
  Have practis'd dangerously against your state,
  Dealing with witches and with conjurers,
  Whom we have apprehended in the fact,
  Raising up wicked spirits from under ground,
  Demanding of King Henry's life and death,   170
  And other of your highness' privy-council ;
  As more at large your grace shall understand.

Car. (*aside to Glo.*) And so, my lord protector, by this
  means

39

Your lady is forthcoming yet at London.
This news, I think, hath turn'd your weapon's edge;
'Tis like, my lord, you will not keep your hour.

Glo. Ambitious churchman, leave to afflict my heart:
Sorrow and grief have vanquish'd all my powers;
And, vanquish'd as I am, I yield to thee,
Or to the meanest groom.   180

King. O God, what mischiefs work the wicked ones,
Heaping confusion on their own heads thereby!

Mar. Gloucester, see here the tainture of thy nest,
And look thyself be faultless, thou wert best.

Glo. Madam, for myself, to heaven I do appeal,
How I have lov'd my king and commonweal:
And for my wife, I know not how it stands;
Sorry I am to hear what I have heard:
Noble she is; but if she have forgot
Honour and virtue, and convers'd with such   190
As, like to pitch, defile nobility,
I banish her my bed and company,
And give her as a prey to law and shame,
That hath dishonour'd Gloucester's honest name.

King. Well, for this night we will repose us here:
To-morrow toward London back again,
To look into this business thoroughly,
And call these foul offenders to their answers,

And poise the cause in justice' equal scales,
Whose beam stands sure, whose rightful cause pre-
    vails.   *Flourish.   Exeunt* 200

SCENE II

London.   The Duke of York's garden

Enter York, Salisbury, and Warwick

Yo. Now, my good Lords of Salisbury and Warwick,
   Our simple supper ended, give me leave
   In this close walk to satisfy myself,
   In craving your opinion of my title,
   Which is infallible, to England's crown.

Sal. My lord, I long to hear it at full.

War. Sweet York, begin : and if thy claim be good,
   The Nevils are thy subjects to command.

Yo. Then thus :
   Edward the Third, my lords, had seven sons :   10
   The first, Edward the Black Prince, Prince of Wales ;
   The second, William of Hatfield ; and the third,
   Lionel, Duke of Clarence ; next to whom
   Was John of Gaunt, the Duke of Lancaster ;
   The fifth was Edmund Langley, Duke of York ;
   The sixth was Thomas of Woodstock, Duke of
       Gloucester ;

41

William of Windsor was the seventh and last.
Edward the Black Prince died before his father,
And left behind him Richard, his only son,
Who after Edward the Third's death reign'd as king,   20
Till Henry Bolingbroke, Duke of Lancaster,
The eldest son and heir of John of Gaunt,
Crown'd by the name of Henry the Fourth,
Seiz'd on the realm, depos'd the rightful king,
Sent his poor queen to France, from whence she came,
And him to Pomfret ; where, as all you know,
Harmless Richard was murder'd traitorously.

*War.*Father, the duke hath told the truth ;
Thus got the house of Lancaster the crown.

Yo. Which now they hold by force and not by right ;   30
For Richard, the first son's heir, being dead,
The issue of the next son should have reign'd.

Sal. But William of Hatfield died without an heir.

Yo. The third son, Duke of Clarence, from whose line
I claim the crown, had issue, Philippe, a daughter,
Who married Edmund Mortimer, Earl of March :
Edmund had issue, Roger, Earl of March ;
Roger had issue, Edmund, Anne and Eleanor.

Sal. This Edmund, in the reign of Bolingbroke,
As I have read, laid claim unto the crown,
And but for Owen Glendower, had been king,   40

Who kept him in captivity till he died.
But to the rest.

Yo.   His eldest sister, Anne,
My mother, being heir unto the crown,
Married Richard Earl of Cambridge ; who was son
To Edmund Langley, Edward the Third's fifth son.
By her I claim the kingdom : she was heir
To Roger, Earl of March, who was the son
Of Edmund Mortimer, who married Philippe,
Sole daughter unto Lionel Duke of Clarence :   50
So, if the issue of the elder son
Succeed before the younger, I am king.

*War.*What plain proceeding is more plain than this ?
Henry doth claim the crown from John of Gaunt,
The fourth son ; York claims it from the third.
Till Lionel's issue fails, his should not reign :
It fails not yet, but flourishes in thee,
And in thy sons, fair slips of such a stock.
Then, father Salisbury, kneel we together,
And in this private plot be we the first   60
That shall salute our rightful sovereign
With honour of his birthright to the crown.

*Both.*Long live our sovereign Richard, England's king !

Yo. We thank you, lords.   But I am not your king
Till I be crown'd, and that my sword be stain'd

With heart-blood of the house of Lancaster;
{And that 's not suddenly to be perform'd,
But with advice and silent secrecy.
Do you as I do in these dangerous days:
Wink at the Duke of Suffolk's insolence,
At Beaufort's pride, at Somerset's ambition,
At Buckingham, and all the crew of them,
Till they have snar'd the shepherd of the flock,
That virtuous prince, the good Duke Humphrey:
'Tis that they seek, and they in seeking that
Shall find their deaths, if York can prophesy.

Sal. My lord, break we off; we know your mind at
full.

War. My heart assures me that the Earl of Warwick
Shall one day make the Duke of York a king.}

[*War.* Then York, advise thyself and take thy time,
Claim thou the crown, and set thy standard up,
And in the same advance the milk-white rose,
And then to guard it will I rouse the bear,
Inviron'd with ten thousand ragged staves,
To aid and help thee for to win thy right,
Maugre the proudest lord of Henry's blood
That dares deny the right and claim of York;
For why my mind presageth I shall live
To see the noble Duke of York to be a king.]

44

o. And, Nevil, this I do assure myself :   80
    Richard shall live to make the Earl of Warwick
    The greatest man in England but the king.   *Exeunt*

SCENE III

A hall of justice

ound trumpets.   Enter the King, the Queen, Gloucester, York,
    Suffolk, and Salisbury ;   the Duchess of Gloucester,
    Margery Jourdain, Southwell, Hume, and Bolingbroke,
    under guard

*ing.*Stand forth, Dame Eleanor Cobham, Gloucester's
    wife :
    In sight of God, and us, your guilt is great :
    Receive the sentence of the law for sins
    Such as by God's book are adjudg'd to death.
    You four, from hence to prison, back again ;
    From thence unto the place of execution :
    The witch in Smithfield shall be burn'd to ashes,
    And you three shall be strangled on the gallows.
    You, madam, for you are more nobly born,
    Despoiled of your honour in your life,   10
    Shall, {after three days' open penance done,   †
    Live in your country here, in banishment,

With Sir John Stanley, in the Isle of Man.}
[two days in London do penance barefoot in the
streets, with a white sheet about thy body, and a wax
taper burning in thy hand.   That done, thou shalt
be banished for ever unto the Isle of Man, there to
end thy wretched days, and this is our sentence
irrevocable.   Away with her !]

Ele. Welcome is banishment ; welcome were my death.

Glo. Eleanor, the law, thou see'st, hath judged thee,
I cannot justify whom the law condemns.

    Exeunt Duchess and other prisoners, guarded
Mine eyes are full of tears, my heart of grief.
Ah, Humphrey, this dishonour in thine age
Will bring thy head with sorrow to the ground !
I beseech your majesty, give me leave to go ;
Sorrow would solace, and mine age would ease. 20

King. Stay, Humphrey Duke of Gloucester, ere thou go,
Give up thy staff : Henry will to himself
Protector be ; and God shall be my hope,
My stay, my guide, and lantern to my feet :
And go in peace, Humphrey, no less belov'd
Than when thou wert protector to thy king.

Mar. I see no reason why a king of years
Should be to be protected like a child.
God and King Henry govern England's realm. 30

46

Give up your staff, sir, and the king his realm.

Glo. My staff? here, noble Henry, is my staff:
As willingly do I the same resign
As e'er thy father Henry made it mine;
And even as willingly at thy feet I leave it
As others would ambitiously receive it.
Farewell, good king: when I am dead and gone,
May honourable peace attend thy throne!   *Exit*

Mar. Why, now is Henry king, and Margaret queen,
And Humphrey Duke of Gloucester scarce himself,   40
That bears so shrewd a maim; two pulls at once;
His lady banish'd, and a limb lopp'd off.
This staff of honour raught, there let it stand
Where it best fits to be, in Henry's hand.

Suf. Thus droops this lofty pine, and hangs his sprays;
Thus Eleanor's pride dies in her youngest days.

Yo. Lords, let him go.   Please it your majesty,
This is the day appointed for the combat,
And ready are the appellant and defendant,
The armourer and his man, to enter the lists   50
So please your highness to behold the fight.

Mar. Ay, good my lord; for purposely therefore
Left I the court, to see this quarrel tried.

King. O' God's name, see the lists and all things fit:
Here let them end it, and God defend the right!

Yo. I never saw a fellow worse bested,
  Or more afraid to fight, than is the appellant,
  The servant of this armourer, my lords.

Enter at one door, Horner, the Armourer, and his Neighbours, drinking to him so much that he is drunk ; and he enters with a drum before him, and his staff with a sand-bag fastened to it ; and at the other door Peter, his man, wtih a drum and sand-bag, and 'Prentices drinking to him

1.*N.* Here, neighbour Horner, I drink to you in a cup of sack : and fear not, neighbour, you shall do well enough.

2.*N.* And here, neighbour, here 's a cup of charneco.

3.*N.* And here 's a pot of good double beer, neighbour : drink, and fear not your man.

Hor. Let it come, i' faith, and I 'll pledge you all, and a fig for Peter !

1.*P.* Here, Peter, I drink to thee, and be not afraid.

2.*P.* Be merry, Peter, and fear not thy master : fight for credit of the 'prentices.

Pet. I thank you all : drink, and pray for me, I pray you, for I think I have taken my last draught in this world. Here, Robin, an if I die, I give thee my apron : and, Will, thou shalt have my hammer : and here, Tom, take all the money that I have. O Lord bless me ! I pray God ! for I am never able to

deal with my master, he hath learnt so much fence
already.

Sal. Come, leave your drinking, and fall to blows.
Sirrah, what's thy name?

Pet. Peter, forsooth.   80

Sal. Peter? what more?

Pet. Thump.

Sal. Thump? then see thou thump thy master well.

Hor. Masters, I am come hither, as it were, upon my
man's instigation, to prove him a knave and myself
an honest man: and touching the Duke of York,
I will take my death, I never meant him any ill, nor
the king, nor the queen: and therefore, Peter, have
at thee with a downright blow! [as Bevis of †
Southampton fell upon Askapart.]

Yo. Dispatch: this knave's tongue begins to double.   91
Sound, trumpets, alarum to the combatants!

>   *Alarum.   They fight, and Peter strikes him down*

Hor. Hold, Peter, hold! I confess, I confess, treason.

>   *Dies*

Yo. Take away his weapon. Fellow, thank God, and
the good wine in thy master's way.

Pet. O God, have I overcome mine enemies in this
presence?   O Peter, thou hast prevail'd in right!

[Prentices. Ho, well done, Peter! God save the king!]

King. Go, take hence that traitor from our sight,
　　　For by his death we do perceive his guilt,　　　　　　100
　　　And God in justice hath reveal'd to us
　　　The truth and innocence of this poor fellow,
　　　Which he had thought to have murder'd wrongfully.
　　　Come, fellow, follow us for thy reward.

　　　　　　　　　　　　Sound a flourish.   Exeunt

SCENE IV

A street

Enter Gloucester, and his Serving-men [in mourning cloaks]

Glo. Thus sometimes hath the brightest day a cloud ;
　　　And after summer, evermore succeeds
　　　Barren winter, with his wrathful nipping cold :
　　　So cares and joys abound, as seasons fleet.
　　　Sirs, what's o'clock ?

Ser.　　　　　　　　　　Ten, my lord.

Glo. Ten is the hour that was appointed me
　　　To watch the coming of my punish'd duchess :
　　　Uneath may she endure the flinty streets,
　　　To tread them with her tender-feeling feet.
　　　Sweet Nell, ill can thy noble mind abrook　　　　　　10
　　　The abject people gazing on thy face,

With envious looks laughing at thy shame,
That erst did follow thy proud chariot-wheels,
When thou didst ride in triumph through the streets.
But, soft ! I think she comes, and I 'll prepare
My tear-stain'd eyes to see her miseries.

Enter the Duchess of Gloucester in a white sheet, and a wax
candle burning in her hand [and verses written on her back
and pinned on] ; with Sir John Stanley, the Sheriff, and
Officers [, with bills and halberds].

Ser. So please your grace, we 'll take her from the sheriff.

Glo. No, stir not for your lives, let her pass by.

Ele. Come you, my lord, to see my open shame ?
Now thou dost penance too.   Look how they gaze !   20
See how the giddy multitude do point,
And nod their heads, and throw their eyes on thee !
Ah, Gloucester, hide thee from their hateful looks,
And, in thy closet pent up, rue my shame,
And ban thine enemies, both mine and thine !

Glo. Be patient, gentle Nell ; forget this grief.

Ele. Ah, Gloucester, teach me to forget myself !
For whilst I think I am thy married wife,
And thou a prince, protector of this land,
Methinks I should not thus be led along,   30
Mail'd up in shame, with papers on my back,
And follow'd with a rabble, that rejoice

To see my tears, and hear my deep-fet groans.
The ruthless flint doth cut my tender feet,
And when I start, the envious people laugh,
And bid me be advised how I tread.
Ah, Humphrey, can I bear this shameful yoke?
Trow'st thou that e'er I'll look upon the world,
Or count them happy that enjoy the sun?
No; dark shall be my light and night my day;   40
To think upon my pomp shall be my hell.
Sometime I'll say, I am Duke Humphrey's wife,
And he a prince, and ruler of the land:
Yet so he rul'd, and such a prince he was,
As he stood by, whilst I, his forlorn duchess,
Was made a wonder, and a pointing-stock
To every idle rascal follower.
But be thou mild, and blush not at my shame,
Nor stir at nothing till the axe of death
Hang over thee, as, sure, it shortly will;   50
For Suffolk—he that can do all in all
With her that hateth thee and hates us all—
And York, and impious Beaufort, that false priest,
Have all lim'd bushes to betray thy wings,
And fly thou how thou canst, they'll tangle thee:
But fear not thou, until thy foot be snar'd,
Nor never seek prevention of thy foes.

Glo. Ah, Nell, forbear! thou aimest all awry;
 I must offend, before I be attainted;
 And had I twenty times so many foes,   60
 And each of them had twenty times their power,
 All these could not procure me any scathe,
 So long as I am loyal, true and crimeless.
 Wouldst have me rescue thee from this reproach?
 Why, yet thy scandal were not wip'd away,
 But I in danger for the breach of law.
 Thy greatest help is quiet, gentle Nell:
 I pray thee, sort thy heart to patience;
 These few days' wonder will be quickly worn.

       Enter a Herald

Her. I summon your grace to his majesty's parliament,   70
 Holden at Bury, the first of this next month.

Glo. And my consent ne'er ask'd herein before!
 This is close dealing. Well, I will be there.

          Exit Herald

 My Nell, I take my leave: and, master sheriff,
 Let not her penance exceed the king's commission.

Sher. An't please your grace, here my commission stays,
 And Sir John Stanley is appointed now
 To take her with him to the Isle of Man.

Glo. Must you, Sir John, protect my lady here?

Stan. So am I given in charge, may't please your grace.   80

Glo. Entreat her not the worse in that I pray †
    You use her well : the world may laugh again,
    And I may live to do you kindness if
    You do it her : and so, Sir John, farewell !

Ele. What, gone, my lord, and bid me not farewell ?

Glo. Witness my tears, I cannot stay to speak.

                          Exeunt Gloucester and Serving-men

Ele. Art thou gone too ? all comfort go with thee !
    For none abides with me : my joy is death,—
    Death, at whose name I oft have been afear'd,
    Because I wish'd this world's eternity.   9°
    Stanley, I prithee, go, and take me hence,
    I care not whither, for I beg no favour,
    Only convey me where thou art commanded.

Stan. Why, madam, that is to the Isle of Man,
    There to be us'd according to your state.

Ele. That's bad enough, for I am but reproach :
    And shall I then be us'd reproachfully ?

Stan. Like to a duchess, and Duke Humphrey's lady ;
    According to that state you shall be us'd.

Ele. Sheriff, farewell, and better than I fare,   10°
    Although thou hast been conduct of my shame.

Sher. It is my office ; and, madam, pardon me.

Ele. Ay, ay, farewell, thy office is discharg'd :
    Come, Stanley, shall we go ?

*tan.*Madam, your penance done, throw off this sheet,
    And go we to attire you for our journey.

Ele. My shame will not be shifted with my sheet :
    No, it will hang upon my richest robes,
    And show itself, attire me how I can.
    Go, lead the way ; I long to see my prison.   *Exeunt* 110

Act Third

SCENE 1

The Abbey at Bury St Edmund's

*Sound a Sennet. Enter King, Queen, Cardinal Beaufort,
Suffolk, York, Buckingham, Salisbury and Warwick to
the Parliament*

*King.*I muse my Lord of Gloucester is not come ;
    'Tis not his wont to be the hindmost man,
    Whate'er occasion keeps him from us now.

*Mar.*Can you not see ? or will ye not observe
    The strangeness of his alter'd countenance ?
    With what a majesty he bears himself,
    How insolent of late he is become,
    How proud, how peremptory, and unlike himself ?

We know the time since he was mild and affable,
And if we did but glance a far-off look,   10
Immediately he was upon his knee,
That all the court admir'd him for submission:
But meet him now, and, be it in the morn,
When every one will give the time of day,
He knits his brow, and shows an angry eye,
And passeth by with stiff unbowed knee,
Disdaining duty that to us belongs.
Small curs are not regarded when they grin,
But great men tremble when the lion roars,
And Humphrey is no little man in England.   20
First note that he is near you in descent,
And should you fall, he is the next will mount.
Me seemeth then it is no policy,
Respecting what a rancorous mind he bears,
And his advantage following your decease,
That he should come about your royal person,
Or be admitted to your highness' council.
By flattery hath he won the commons' hearts,
And when he please to make commotion,
'Tis to be fear'd they all will follow him.   30
Now 'tis the spring, and weeds are shallow-rooted;
Suffer them now, and they 'll o'ergrow the garden,
And choke the herbs for want of husbandry.

The reverent care I bear unto my lord
Made me collect these dangers in the duke.
If it be fond, call it a woman's fear;
Which fear if better reasons can supplant,
I will subscribe, and say I wrong'd the duke.
My Lord of Suffolk, Buckingham, and York,
Reprove my allegation, if you can,   40
Or else conclude my words effectual.

Suf. Well hath your highness seen into this duke;
And had I first been put to speak my mind,
I think I should have told your grace's tale.
The duchess by his subornation,
Upon my life, began her devilish practices:
Or, if he were not privy to those faults,
Yet, by reputing of his high descent,
As next the king he was successive heir,
And such high vaunts of his nobility,   50
Did instigate the bedlam brain-sick duchess
By wicked means to frame our sovereign's fall.
Smooth runs the water where the brook is deep,
And in his simple show he harbours treason.
The fox barks not when he would steal the lamb.
No, no, my sovereign, Gloucester is a man
Unsounded yet, and full of deep deceit.

Car. Did he not, contrary to form of law,

57

Devise strange deaths for small offences done?

Yo. And did he not, in his protectorship,   60
Levy great sums of money through the realm
For soldiers' pay in France, and never sent it?
By means whereof the towns each day revolted.

Buc. Tut, these are petty faults to faults unknown,
Which time will bring to light in smooth Duke
    Humphrey.

King. My lords, at once: the care you have of us,
To mow down thorns that would annoy our foot,
Is worthy praise: but, shall I speak my conscience,
Our kinsman Gloucester is as innocent
From meaning treason to our royal person,   70
As is the sucking lamb, or harmless dove:
The duke is virtuous, mild, and too well given
To dream on evil, or to work my downfall.

Mar. Ah, what's more dangerous than this fond affiance?
Seems he a dove? his feathers are but borrow'd,
For he's dispos'd as the hateful raven:
Is he a lamb? his skin is surely lent him,
For he's inclin'd as is the ravenous wolf.
Who cannot steal a shape that means deceit?
Take heed, my lord, the welfare of us all   80
Hangs on the cutting short that fraudful man.

Enter Somerset

Som. All health unto my gracious sovereign !

King. Welcome, Lord Somerset.   What news from France ?

Som. That all your interest in those territories
  Is utterly bereft you ; all is lost.

King. Cold news, Lord Somerset : but God's will be done !

Yo. (*aside*) Cold news for me ; for I had hope of France,
  As firmly as I hope for fertile England.
  Thus are my blossoms blasted in the bud,
  And caterpillars eat my leaves away ;   90
  But I will remedy this gear ere long,
  Or sell my title for a glorious grave.

Enter Gloucester

Glo. All happiness unto my lord the king !
  Pardon, my liege, that I have stay'd so long.

Suf. Nay, Gloucester, know that thou art come too soon,
  Unless thou wert more loyal than thou art :
  I do arrest thee of high treason here.

Glo. Well, Suffolk, thou shalt not see me blush,
  Nor change my countenance for this arrest :
  A heart unspotted is not easily daunted.   100
  The purest spring is not so free from mud
  As I am clear from treason to my sovereign :
  Who can accuse me ? wherein am I guilty ?

Yo. 'Tis thought, my lord, that you took bribes of France,

And, being protector, stay'd the soldiers' pay,
By means whereof his highness hath lost France.

Glo. Is it but thought so? what are they that think it?
I never robb'd the soldiers of their pay,
Nor ever had one penny bribe from France.
So help me God, as I have watch'd the night,   110
Ay, night by night, in studying good for England!
That doit that e'er I wrested from the king,
Or any groat I hoarded to my use,
Be brought against me at my trial-day!   †
No; many a pound of mine own proper store,
Because I would not tax the needy commons,
Have I dispursed to the garrisons,
And never ask'd for restitution.

Car. It serves you well, my lord, to say so much.

Glo. I say no more than truth, so help me God!   120

Yo. In your protectorship, you did devise
Strange tortures for offenders, never heard of,
That England was defam'd by tyranny.

Glo. Why, 'tis well known that, whiles I was protector,
Pity was all the fault that was in me;
For I should melt at an offender's tears,
And lowly words were ransom for their fault.
Unless it were a bloody murderer,
Or foul felonious thief, that fleec'd poor passengers,

I never gave them condign punishment :   130
Murder indeed, that bloody sin, I tortur'd
Above the felon, or what trespass else.

Suf. My lord, these faults are easy, quickly answer'd :
But mightier crimes are laid unto your charge,
Whereof you cannot easily purge yourself.
I do arrest you in his highness' name,
And here commit you to my lord cardinal
To keep, until your further time of trial.

King. My Lord of Gloucester, 'tis my special hope
That you will clear yourself from all suspect : 140
My conscience tells me you are innocent.

Glo. Ah, gracious lord, these days are dangerous :
Virtue is chok'd with foul ambition,
And charity chas'd hence by rancour's hand ;
Foul subornation is predominant,
And equity exil'd your higness' land.
I know their complot is to have my life ;
And if my death might make this island happy,
And prove the period of their tyranny,
I would expend it with all willingness :   150
But mine is made the prologue to their play ;
For thousands more, that yet suspect no peril,
Will not conclude their plotted tragedy.
Beaufort's red sparkling eyes blab his heart's malice,

And Suffolk's cloudy brow his stormy hate;
Sharp Buckingham unburthens with his tongue
The envious load that lies upon his heart;
And dogged York, that reaches at the moon,
Whose overweening arm I have pluck'd back,
By false accuse doth level at my life: 160
And you, my sovereign lady, with the rest,
Causeless have laid disgraces on my head,
And with your best endeavour have stirr'd up
My liefest liege to be mine enemy:
Ay, all of you have laid your heads together—
Myself had notice of your conventicles—
And all to make away my guiltless life.
I shall not want false witness, to condemn me,
Nor store of treasons, to augment my guilt;
The ancient proverb will be well effected: 170
' A staff is quickly found to beat a dog.'

Car. My liege, his railing is intolerable:
If those that care to keep your royal person
From treason's secret knife, and traitors' rage,
Be thus upbraided, chid, and rated at,
And the offender granted scope of speech,
'Twill make them cool in zeal unto your grace.

Suf. Hath he not twit our sovereign lady here
With ignominious words, though clerkly couch'd?

As if she had suborned some to swear   180
False allegations, to o'erthrow his state?

Mar. But I can give the loser leave to chide.

Glo. Far truer spoke than meant: I lose indeed;
Beshrew the winners, for they play'd me false!
And well such losers may have leave to speak.

Buc. He'll wrest the sense, and hold us here all day:
Lord cardinal, he is your prisoner.

Car. Sirs, take away the duke, and guard him sure.

Glo. Ah! thus King Henry throws away his crutch,
Before his legs be firm to bear his body.   190
Thus is the shepherd beaten from thy side,
And wolves are gnarling who shall gnaw thee first.   †
Ah, that my fear were false! ah, that it were!
For, good King Henry, thy decay I fear.

Exit, guarded

King. My lords, what to your wisdoms seemeth best,
Do, or undo, as if ourself were here.

Mar. What, will your highness leave the Parliament?

King. Ay, Margaret; my heart is drown'd with grief,
Whose flood begins to flow within mine eyes,
My body round engirt with misery,   200
For what's more miserable than discontent?
Ah, uncle Humphrey, in thy face I see
The map of honour, truth, and loyalty:

And yet, good Humphrey, is the hour to come
That e'er I prov'd thee false, or fear'd thy faith.
What louring star now envies thy estate,
That these great lords, and Margaret our queen,
Do seek subversion of thy harmless life?
Thou never didst them wrong, nor no man wrong;
And as the butcher takes away the calf,   210
And binds the wretch, and beats it when it strays,
Bearing it to the bloody slaughter-house,
Even so remorseless have they borne him hence;
And as the dam runs lowing up and down,
Looking the way her harmless young one went,
And can do nought but wail her darling's loss,
Even so myself bewails good Gloucester's case
With sad unhelpful tears, and with dimm'd eyes
Look after him, and cannot do him good,
So mighty are his vowed enemies.   220
His fortunes I will weep, and 'twixt each groan
Say 'Who's a traitor?   Gloucester he is none.'

*Exeunt all but Queen, Cardinal Beaufort, Suffolk,
and York.   Somerset remains apart*

*Mar.*Free lords, cold snow melts with the sun's hot beams.
Henry, my lord, is cold in great affairs,
Too full of foolish pity; and Gloucester's show
Beguiles him, as the mournful crocodile   †

With sorrow snares relenting passengers;
Or as the snake, roll'd in a flowering bank,
With shining checker'd slough, doth sting a child,
That for the beauty thinks it excellent.   230
Believe me, lords, were none more wise than I—
And yet herein I judge mine own wit good—
This Gloucester should be quickly rid the world,
To rid us from the fear we have of him.

Car. That he should die is worthy policy,
But yet we want a colour for his death:
'Tis meet he be condemn'd by course of law.

Suf. But, in my mind, that were no policy:
The king will labour still to save his life,
The commons haply rise, to save his life;   240
And yet we have but trivial argument,
More than mistrust, that shows him worthy death.

Yo. So that, by this, you would not have him die.

Suf. Ah, York, no man alive so fain as I!

Yo. 'Tis York that hath more reason for his death.
But, my lord cardinal, and you, my Lord of Suffolk,
Say as you think, and speak it from your souls:
Were't not all one, an empty eagle were set
To guard the chicken from a hungry kite,
As place Duke Humphrey for the king's protector? 250

Mar. So the poor chicken should be sure of death.

Suf. Madam, 'tis true ; and were 't not madness, then,
　　To make the fox surveyor of the fold ?
　　Who being accus'd a crafty murderer,
　　His guilt should be but idly posted over,
　　Because his purpose is not executed.
　　No ; let him die, in that he is a fox,
　　By nature prov'd an enemy to the flock,
　　Before his chaps be stain'd with crimson blood,
　　As Humphrey, prov'd by reasons, to my liege.　　**260**
　　And do not stand on quillets how to slay him :
　　Be it by gins, by snares, by subtlety,
　　Sleeping, or waking, 'tis no matter how,
　　So he be dead ; for that is good deceit
　　Which mates him first that first intends deceit.

Mar. Thrice-noble Suffolk, 'tis resolutely spoke.

Suf. Not resolute, except so much were done,
　　For things are often spoke, and seldom meant :
　　But that my heart accordeth with my tongue,
　　Seeing the deed is meritorious,　　**270**
　　And to preserve my sovereign from his foe,
　　Say but the word, and I will be his priest.

Car. But I would have him dead, my lord of Suffolk,
　　Ere you can take due orders for a priest :
　　Say you consent, and censure well the deed,
　　And I 'll provide his executioner,

66

      I tender so the safety of my liege.

Suf. Here is my hand, the deed is worthy doing.

Mar. And so say I.

Yo. And I: and now we three have spoke it,   280
      It skills not greatly who impugns our doom.

Enter a Post

Post. Great lords, from Ireland am I come amain,   †
      To signify that rebels there are up,
      And put the Englishmen unto the sword :
      Send succours, lords, and stop the rage betime,
      Before the wound do grow uncurable ;
      For, being green, there is great hope of help.

Car. A breach that craves a quick expedient stop !
      What counsel give you in this weighty cause ?

Yo. That Somerset be sent as regent thither :   290
      'Tis meet that lucky ruler be employ'd ;
      Witness the fortune he hath had in France.

Som. If York, with all his far-fet policy,
      Had been the regent there instead of me,
      He never would have stay'd in France so long.

Yo. No, not to lose it all, as thou hast done :
      I rather would have lost my life betimes
      Than bring a burthen of dishonour home,
      By staying there so long, till all were lost.
      Show me one scar character'd on thy skin :   300

Men's flesh preserv'd so whole do seldom win.

Mar. Nay, then, this spark will prove a raging fire,
If wind and fuel be brought, to feed it with :
No more, good York ; sweet Somerset, be still :
Thy fortune, York, hadst thou been regent there,
Might happily have prov'd far worse than his.

Yo. What, worse than nought ? nay, then, a shame take all !

Som. And, in the number, thee, that wishest shame !

Car. My Lord of York, try what your fortune is.
The uncivil kernes of Ireland are in arms,   310
And temper clay with blood of Englishmen :
To Ireland will you lead a band of men,
Collected choicely, from each county some,
And try your hap against the Irishmen ?

Yo. I will, my lord, so please his majesty.

Suf. Why, our authority is his consent,
And what we do establish he confirms.
Then, noble York, take thou this task in hand.

Yo. I am content : provide me soldiers, lords,
Whiles I take order for mine own affairs.   320

Suf. A charge, Lord York, that I will see perform'd.
But now return we to the false Duke Humphrey.

Car. No more of him ; for I will deal with him,
That henceforth he shall trouble us no more.
And so break off, the day is almost spent :

Lord Suffolk, you and I must talk of that event.

Yo. My Lord of Suffolk, within fourteen days
    At Bristol I expect my soldiers;
    For there I'll ship them all for Ireland.

Suf. I'll see it truly done, my Lord of York.   330

Exeunt all but York

Yo. Now, York, or never, steel thy fearful thoughts,
    And change misdoubt to resolution:
    Be that thou hop'st to be, or what thou art
    Resign to death; it is not worth the enjoying:
    Let pale-fac'd fear keep with the mean-born man,
    And find no harbour in a royal heart.
    Faster than spring-time showers comes thought on
        thought,
    And not a thought but thinks on dignity.
    My brain more busy than the labouring spider
    Weaves tedious snares to trap mine enemies.   340
    Well, nobles, well; 'tis politicly done,
    To send me packing with an host of men:
    I fear me, you but warm the starved snake.
    Who, cherish'd in your breasts, will sting your hearts.
    'Twas men I lack'd, and you will give them me:
    I take it kindly; yet be well assur'd
    You put sharp weapons in a madman's hands.
    Whiles I in Ireland nourish a mighty band,

I will stir up in England some black storm
Shall blow ten thousand souls to heaven, or hell;   35(
And this fell tempest shall not cease to rage
Until the golden circuit on my head,
Like to the glorious sun's transparent beams,
Do calm the fury of this mad-bred flaw.
And, for a minister of my intent,
I have seduc'd a headstrong Kentishman,
John Cade of Ashford,
To make commotion, as full well he can,
Under the title of John Mortimer.
In Ireland have I seen this stubborn Cade   36(
Oppose himself against a troop of kernes,
And fought so long, till that his thighs with darts
Were almost like a sharp-quill'd porpentine;
And, in the end being rescued, I have seen
Him caper upright, like a wild Morisco,
Shaking the bloody darts as he his bells.
Full often, like a shag-hair'd crafty kerne,
Hath he conversed with the enemy,
And undiscover'd come to me again,
And given me notice of their villanies.   37
This devil here shall be my substitute;
For that John Mortimer, which now is dead,
In face, in gait, in speech, he doth resemble:

By this I shall perceive the commons' mind,
How they affect the house and claim of York
Say he be taken, rack'd and tortured,
I know no pain they can inflict upon him
Will make him say I mov'd him to those arms.
Say that he thrive, as 'tis great like he will,
Why, then from Ireland come I with my strength,   380
And reap the harvest which that rascal sow'd ;
For Humphrey being dead, as he shall be,
And Henry put apart, the next for me.   *Exit*

SCENE II

Bury St Edmund's.   A room of state

Enter certain Murderers, hastily   †

1.M. Run to my Lord of Suffolk ; let him know
We have dispatch'd the duke, as he commanded.
2.M. O, that it were to do ! what have we done ?
Didst ever hear a man so penitent ?

Enter Suffolk

1.M. Here comes my lord.
Suf. Now, sirs, have you dispatch'd this thing ?
1.M. Ay, my good lord, he 's dead.
Suf. Why, that 's well said.   Go, get you to my house,

I will reward you for this venturous deed.
The king and all the peers are here at hand.   I●
Have you laid fair the bed ?   Is all things well,
According as I gave directions ?

1.M.'Tis, my good lord.

Suf. Away, be gone !   *Exeunt Murderers*
    *Sound trumpets.   Enter the King, the Queen, Cardinal
        Beaufort, Somerset, with Attendants*

*King.*Go, call our uncle to our presence straight ;
    Say, we intend to try his grace to-day,
    If he be guilty, as 'tis published.

Suf. I 'll call him presently, my noble lord.   *Exit*

*King.*Lords, take your places ; and I pray you all
    Proceed no straiter 'gainst our uncle Gloucester   2●
    Than from true evidence, of good esteem,
    He be approv'd in practice culpable.

*Mar.*God forbid any malice should prevail,
    That faultless may condemn a nobleman !
    Pray God he may acquit him of suspicion !

*King.*I thank thee, Nell ; these words content me much. †
                    Re-enter Suffolk
    How now ? why look'st thou pale ? why tremblest
        thou ?
    Where is our uncle ? what's the matter, Suffolk ?

Suf. Dead in his bed, my lord ; Gloucester is dead.

*Mar.*Marry, God forfend !   30
Car. God's secret judgement : I did dream to-night
    The duke was dumb, and could not speak a word.

                                    The King swoons

*Mar.*How fares my lord ? Help, lords ! the king is dead.
Som. Rear up his body, wring him by the nose.
*Mar.*Run, go, help, help !   O Henry, ope thine eyes !
Suf. He doth revive again : madam, be patient.
*King.*O heavenly God !
Mar.   How fares my gracious lord ?
Suf. Comfort, my sovereign ! gracious Henry, comfort !
*King.*What, doth my Lord of Suffolk comfort me ?
    Came he right now to sing a raven's note,   40
    Whose dismal tune bereft my vital powers ;
    And thinks he that the chirping of a wren,
    By crying comfort from a hollow breast,
    Can chase away the first-conceived sound ?
    Hide not thy poison with such sugar'd words,
    Lay not thy hands on me ; forbear, I say,
    Their touch affrights me as a serpent's sting.
    Thou baleful messenger, out of my sight !
    Upon thy eye-balls murderous tyranny
    Sits in grim majesty, to fright the world.   50
    Look not upon me, for thine eyes are wounding :
    Yet do not go away : come, basilisk,

                      73

And kill the innocent gazer with thy sight ;
For in the shade of death I shall find joy ;
In life but double death, now Gloucester's dead.

Mar. Why do you rate my Lord of Suffolk thus ?
Although the duke was enemy to him,
Yet he most Christian-like laments his death :
And for myself, foe as he was to me,
Might liquid tears, or heart-offending groans, 60
Or blood-consuming sighs recall his life,
I would be blind with weeping, sick with groans,
Look pale as primrose with blood-drinking sighs,
And all to have the noble duke alive.
What know I how the world may deem of me ?
For it is known we were but hollow friends :
It may be judg'd I made the duke away,
So shall my name with slander's tongue be wounded,
And princes' courts be fill'd with my reproach.
This get I by his death : ay me unhappy, 70
To be a queen, and crown'd with infamy !

King. Ah, woe is me for Gloucester, wretched man !

Mar. Be woe for me, more wretched than he is.
What, dost thou turn away and hide thy face ?
I am no loathsome leper ; look on me.
What ? art thou like the adder waxen deaf ?
Be poisonous too, and kill thy forlorn queen.

Is all thy comfort shut in Gloucester's tomb?
Why, then, dame Eleanor was ne'er thy joy.
Erect his statuĕ, and worship it,　　　　　　80
And make my image but an alehouse sign.
Was I for this nigh wreck'd upon the sea,
And twice by awkward wind from England's bank
Drove back again unto my native clime?
What boded this, but well forewarning wind
Did seem to say 'Seek not a scorpion's nest,
Nor set no footing on this unkind shore'?
What did I then? but curs'd the gentle gusts,
And he that loos'd them forth their brazen caves;
And bid them blow towards England's blessed shore,　90
Or turn our stern upon a dreadful rock?
Yet Æolus would not be a murderer,
But left that hateful office unto thee:
The pretty vaulting sea refus'd to drown me,
Knowing that thou would'st have me drown'd on
　　　shore,
With tears as salt as sea, through thy unkindness:
The splitting rocks cower'd in the sinking sands,
And would not dash me with their ragged sides,
Because thy flinty heart, more hard than they,
Might in thy palace perish Margaret.　　　　　100
As far as I could ken thy chalky cliffs

When from thy shore the tempest beat us back,
I stood upon the hatches in the storm ;
And when the dusky sky began to rob
My earnest-gaping sight of thy land's view,
I took a costly jewel from my neck—
A heart it was, bound in with diamonds—
And threw it towards thy land : the sea receiv'd it,
And so I wish'd thy body might my heart :
And even with this I lost fair England's view, 110
And bid mine eyes be packing with my heart,
And call'd them blind and dusky spectacles,
For losing ken of Albion's wished coast.
How often have I tempted Suffolk's tongue,
(The agent of thy foul inconstancy)
To sit and witch me, as Ascanius did, †
When he to madding Dido would unfold
His father's acts, commenc'd in burning Troy !
Am I not witch'd like her ? or thou not false like
him ?
Ay me, I can no more ! die, Margaret ! 120
For Henry weeps that thou dost live so long.

*Noise within.   Enter Warwick, Salisbury, and
many Commons*

War. It is reported, mighty sovereign,
That good Duke Humphrey traitorously is murder'd

By Suffolk and the Cardinal Beaufort's means.
The commons, like an angry hive of bees
That want their leader, scatter up and down,
And care not who they sting in his revenge.
Myself have calm'd their spleenful mutiny,
Until they hear the order of his death.

King. That he is dead, good Warwick, 'tis too true,   130
But how he died God knows, not Henry :
Enter his chamber, view his breathless corpse,
And comment then upon his sudden death.

War. That shall I do, my liege.   Stay, Salisbury,
With the rude multitude, till I return.   *Exit*

King. O Thou that judgest all things, stay my thoughts ;
My thoughts, that labour to persuade my soul
Some violent hands were laid on Humphrey's life !
If my suspect be false, forgive me, God,
For judgement only doth belong to Thee.   140
Fain would I go to chafe his paly lips
With twenty thousand kisses, and to drain
Upon his face an ocean of salt tears,
To tell my love unto his dumb deaf trunk,
And with my fingers feel his hand unfeeling :
But all in vain are these mean obsequies ;
And to survey his dead and earthy image,
What were it but to make my sorrow greater ?

*Re-enter Warwick and others, bearing Gloucester's
body on a bed*

War. Come hither, gracious sovereign, view this body.

King. That is to see how deep my grave is made,　　　150
　　For with his soul fled all my worldly solace,
　　For seeing him I see my life in death.

War. As surely as my soul intends to live
　　With that dread King, that took our state upon him,
　　To free us from his Father's wrathful curse,
　　I do believe that violent hands were laid
　　Upon the life of this thrice-famed duke.

Suf. A dreadful oath, sworn with a solemn tongue !
　　What instance gives Lord Warwick for his vow ?

War. See how the blood is settled in his face.　　　160
　　Oft have I seen a timely-parted ghost,
　　Of ashy semblance, meagre, pale, and bloodless
　　Being all descended to the labouring heart ;
　　Who, in the conflict that it holds with death,
　　Attracts the same for aidance 'gainst the enemy ;
　　Which with the heart there cools, and ne'er returneth
　　To blush and beautify the cheek again.
　　But see, his face is black, and full of blood,
　　His eye-balls further out than when he liv'd,
　　Staring full ghastly, like a strangled man ;　　　170
　　His hair uprear'd, his nostrils stretch'd with struggling ;

His hands abroad display'd, as one that grasp'd
And tugg'd for life, and was by strength subdued :
Look, on the sheets his hair, you see, is sticking ;
His well-proportion'd beard made rough and rugged,
Like to the summer's corn by tempest lodged.
It cannot be but he was murder'd here ;
The least of all these signs were probable.

Suf. Why, Warwick, who should do the duke to death ?
  Myself and Beaufort had him in protection ;   180
  And we, I hope, sir, are no murderers.

War. But both of you were vow'd Duke Humphrey's foes,
  And you, forsooth, had the good duke to keep :
  'Tis like you would not feast him like a friend,
  And 'tis well seen he found an enemy.

Mar. Then you, belike, suspect these noblemen
  As guilty of Duke Humphrey's timeless death.

War. Who finds the heifer dead, and bleeding fresh,
  And sees fast by a butcher with an axe,
  But will suspect 'twas he that made the slaughter ?   190
  Who finds the partridge in the puttock's nest,
  But may imagine how the bird was dead,   †
  Although the kite soar with unbloodied beak ?
  Even so suspicious is this tragedy.

Mar. Are you the butcher, Suffolk ?   Where 's your knife ?
  Is Beaufort term'd a kite ?   Where are his talons ?

Suf. I wear no knife to slaughter sleeping men,
But here's a vengeful sword, rusted with ease,
That shall be scoured in his rancorous heart
That slanders me with murder's crimson badge.   200
Say, if thou dar'st, proud Lord of Warwickshire,
That I am faulty in Duke Humphrey's death.

Exeunt Cardinal, Somerset, and others

War. What dares not Warwick, if false Suffolk dare him?

Mar. He dares not calm his contumelious spirit,
Nor cease to be an arrogant controller,
Though Suffolk dare him twenty thousand times.

War. Madam, be still; with reverence may I say,
For every word you speak in his behalf
Is slander to your royal dignity.

Suf. Blunt-witted lord, ignoble in demeanour!   210
If ever lady wrong'd her lord so much,
Thy mother took into her blameful bed
Some stern untutor'd churl; and noble stock
Was graft with crab-tree slip, whose fruit thou art,
And never of the Nevils' noble race.

War. But that the guilt of murder bucklers thee,
And I should rob the deathsman of his fee,
Quitting thee thereby of ten thousand shames,
And that my sovereign's presence makes me mild,
I would, false murderous coward, on thy knee   220

Make thee beg pardon for thy passed speech,
And say it was thy mother that thou meant'st,
That thou thyself wast born in bastardy;
And after all this fearful homage done,
Give thee thy hire, and send thy soul to hell,
Pernicious blood-sucker of sleeping men!

Suf. Thou shalt be waking while I shed thy blood,
If from this presence thou dar'st go with me.

War. Away even now, or I will drag thee hence:
Unworthy though thou art, I'll cope with thee,   230
And do some service to Duke Humphrey's ghost.
                              Exeunt Suffolk and Warwick

King. What stronger breastplate than a heart untainted?
Thrice is he arm'd that hath his quarrel just,
And he but naked, though lock'd up in steel,
Whose conscience with injustice is corrupted.
                                        A noise within

Mar. What noise is this?
           *Re-enter Suffolk and Warwick, with their weapons
                            drawn*

King. Why, how now, lords? your wrathful weapons
              drawn
Here in our presence? dare you be so bold?
Why, what tumultuous clamour have we here?

Suf. The traitorous Warwick, with the men of Bury,   240

Set all upon me, mighty sovereign.

Sal. (*to the Commons, entering*) Sirs, stand apart ; the king
     shall know your mind.
Dread lord, the commons send you word by me,
Unless Lord Suffolk straight be done to death,
Or banished fair England's territories,
They will by violence tear him from your palace,
And torture him with grievous lingering death.
They say, by him the good Duke Humphrey died ;
They say, in him they fear your highness' death ;
And mere instinct of love and loyalty,   250
Free from a stubborn opposite intent,
As being thought to contradict your liking,
Makes them thus forward in his banishment.
They say, in care of your most royal person,
That if your highness should intend to sleep,
And charge that no man should disturb your rest
In pain of your dislike, or pain of death,
Yet, notwithstanding such a strait edict,
Were there a serpent seen, with forked tongue,
That slily glided towards your majesty,   260
It were but necessary you were wak'd,
Lest, being suffer'd in that harmful slumber,
The mortal worm might make the sleep eternal ;
And therefore do they cry, though you forbid,

That they will guard you, whether you will or no,
From such fell serpents as false Suffolk is,
With whose envenomed and fatal sting,
Your loving uncle, twenty times his worth,
They say, is shamefully bereft of life.

Commons (*within*). An answer from the king, my Lord of
    Salisbury!   270

Suf. 'Tis like the commons, rude unpolish'd hinds,
Could send such message to their sovereign:
But you, my lord, were glad to be employ'd,
To show how quaint an orator you are:
But all the honour Salisbury hath won
Is, that he was the lord ambassador
Sent from a sort of tinkers to the king.

Commons (*within*). An answer from the king, or we will
    all break in!

King. Go, Salisbury, and tell them all from me,
I thank them for their tender loving care;   280
And had I not been cited so by them,
Yet did I purpose as they do entreat;
For, sure, my thoughts do hourly prophesy
Mischance unto my state by Suffolk's means;
And therefore, by His majesty I swear,
Whose far unworthy deputy I am,
He shall not breathe infection in this air

But three days longer, on the pain of death.

Exit Salisbury

*Mar.*O Henry, let me plead for gentle Suffolk!

*King.*Ungentle queen, to call him gentle Suffolk!　　　　290
　　No more, I say: if thou dost plead for him,
　　Thou wilt but add increase unto my wrath.
　　Had I but said, I would have kept my word;
　　But when I swear, it is irrevocable.
　　If after three days' space thou here be'st found,
　　On any ground that I am ruler of,
　　The world shall not be ransom for thy life.
　　Come, Warwick, come, good Warwick, go with me,
　　I have great matters to impart to thee.

Exeunt all but Queen and Suffolk

*Mar.*Mischance and sorrow go along with you,　　　　†
　　Heart's discontent and sour affliction　　　　301
　　Be playfellows to keep you company!
　　There's two of you, the devil make a third,
　　And threefold vengeance tend upon your steps!

Suf. Cease, gentle queen, these execrations,
　　And let thy Suffolk take his heavy leave.

*Mar.*Fie, coward woman, and soft-hearted wretch,
　　Hast thou not spirit to curse thine enemy?

Suf. A plague upon them! wherefore should I curse them?
　　Would curses kill, as doth the mandrake's groan,　　　　†

I would invent as bitter-searching terms,   311
As curst, as harsh, and horrible to hear,
Deliver'd strongly through my fixed teeth,
With full as many signs of deadly hate,
As lean-fac'd Envy in her loathsome cave :   †
My tongue should stumble in mine earnest words,
Mine eyes should sparkle like the beaten flint,
Mine hair be fix'd an end, as one distract ;
Ay, every joint should seem to curse and ban,
And even now my burthen'd heart would break,   320
Should I not curse them.   Poison be their drink !
Gall, worse than gall, the daintiest that they taste !
Their sweetest shade, a grove of cypress trees !
Their chiefest prospect, murdering basilisks !
Their softest touch, as smart as lizards' stings !
Their music, frightful as the serpent's hiss,
And boding screech-owls make the concert full !
All the foul terrors in dark-seated hell—

Mar. Enough, sweet Suffolk, thou torment'st thyself,
And these dread curses, like the sun 'gainst glass,   330
Or like an overcharged gun, recoil,
And turn the force of them upon thyself.

Suf. You bade me ban, and will you bid me leave ?
Now by the ground that I am banish'd from,
Well could I curse away a winter's night,

Though standing naked on a mountain top,
Where biting cold would never let grass grow,
And think it but a minute spent in sport.

*Mar.*O, let me entreat thee cease ; give me thy hand,
That I may dew it with my mournful tears ;
Nor let the rain of heaven wet this place,
To wash away my woful monuments.
O, could this kiss be printed in thy hand,
That thou mightst think upon them by the seal,
Through whom a thousand sighs are breath'd for
    thee !
So, get thee gone, that I may know my grief ;
'Tis but surmis'd, whiles thou art standing by,
As one that surfeits, thinking on a want.
I will repeal thee, or, be well assur'd,
Adventure to be banished myself :
And banished I am, if but from thee.
Go, speak not to me ; even now be gone.
O go not yet ! Even thus two friends condemn'd
Embrace, and kiss, and take ten thousand leaves,
Loather a hundred times to part than die ;
Yet now farewell, and farewell life with thee !

Suf. Thus is poor Suffolk ten times banished ;
Once by the king, and three times thrice by thee.
'Tis not the land I care for, wert thou thence ;

A wilderness is populous enough,
So Suffolk had thy heavenly company:
For where thou art, there is the world itself,
With every several pleasure in the world,
And where thou art not, desolation.
I can no more: live thou to joy thy life;
Myself no joy in nought but that thou liv'st.

Enter Vaux

Mar. Whither goes Vaux so fast? what news, I prithee?

Vaux. To signify unto his majesty
That Cardinal Beaufort is at point of death;
For suddenly a grievous sickness took him,   370
That makes him gasp, and stare, and catch the air,
Blaspheming God, and cursing men on earth.
Sometime he talks as if Duke Humphrey's ghost
Were by his side; sometime he calls the king,
And whispers to his pillow, as to him,
The secrets of his overcharged soul,
And I am sent to tell his majesty,
That even now he cries aloud for him.

Mar. Go tell this heavy message to the king.   *Exit Vaux*
Ay me! what is this world? what news are these? 380
But wherefore grieve I at an hour's poor loss,
Omitting Suffolk's exile, my soul's treasure?
Why only, Suffolk, mourn I not for thee?

And with the southern clouds contend in tears?
Theirs for the earth's increase, mine for my sorrows?
Now get thee hence, the king, thou know'st, is
    coming,
If thou be found by me, thou art but dead.

Suf. If I depart from thee, I cannot live,
And in thy sight to die, what were it else
But like a pleasant slumber in thy lap?
Here could I breathe my soul into the air,
As mild and gentle as the cradle-babe,
Dying with mother's dug between its lips:
Where, from thy sight, I should be raging mad,
And cry out for thee to close up mine eyes,
To have thee with thy lips to stop my mouth;
So should'st thou either turn my flying soul,
Or I should breathe it so into thy body,
And then it liv'd in sweet Elysium.
To die by thee were but to die in jest;
From thee to die were torture more than death:
O let me stay, befall what may befall!

Mar. Away!
Though parting be a fretful corrosive,
It is applied to a deathful wound.
To France, sweet Suffolk: let me hear from thee;
For wheresoe'er thou art in this world's globe,

390

400

I'll have an Iris that shall find thee out.

Suf. I go.

Mar.   And take my heart with thee.

Suf. A jewel, lock'd into the wofull'st cask   410
    That ever did contain a thing of worth.
    Even as a splitted bark, so sunder we :
    This way fall I to death.

Mar.   This way for me.

                    Exeunt severally

SCENE III

{*Enter the King, Salisbury, Warwick, to the Cardinal
in bed*}

[*Enter King and Salisbury, and then the curtains be drawn,
and the Cardinal is discovered in his bed, raving and
staring as if he were mad*]

*King.*How fares my lord ? speak, Beaufort, to thy sovereign.

Car. If thou be'st death, I'll give thee England's treasure,
    Enough to purchase such another island,
    So thou wilt let me live, and feel no pain.

*King.*Ah, what a sign it is of evil life,
    Where death's approach is seen so terrible !

*War.*Beaufort, it is thy sovereign speaks to thee.

Car. Bring me unto my trial when you will.

Died he not in his bed ? where should he die ?
Can I make men live, whether they will or no ?   10
O, torture me no more, I will confess.
Alive again ? then show me where he is,
I'll give a thousand pound to look upon him.
He hath no eyes, the dust hath blinded them.
Comb down his hair ; look, look, it stands upright,
Like lime-twigs set to catch my winged soul.
Give me some drink, and bid the apothecary
Bring the strong poison that I bought of him.

King. O thou eternal mover of the heavens,
Look with a gentle eye upon this wretch !   20
O beat away the busy meddling fiend,
That lays strong siege unto this wretch's soul,
And from his bosom purge this black despair !

War. See, how the pangs of death do make him grin !

Sal. Disturb him not, let him pass peaceably.

King. Peace to his soul, if God's good pleasure be !
Lord cardinal, if thou think'st on heaven's bliss,
Hold up thy hand, make signal of thy hope.
He dies, and makes no sign. O God, forgive him !

War. So bad a death argues a monstrous life.   30

King. Forbear to judge, for we are sinners all.
Close up his eyes, and draw the curtain close ;
And let us all to meditation.   *Exeunt*

Act Fourth

SCENE I

The coast of Kent

Alarum. Fight at sea. Ordnance goes off. Enter a Captain, †
a Master, a Master's-Mate, Walter Whitmore, and
others ; with them Suffolk, and others, prisoners

Cap. The gaudy, blabbing, and remorseful day
    Is crept into the bosom of the sea ;
    And now loud-howling wolves arouse the jades
    That drag the tragic melancholy night ;
    Who, with their drowsy, slow, and flagging wings,
    Clip dead men's graves, and from their misty jaws
    Breathe foul contagious darkness in the air.
    Therefore bring forth the soldiers of our prize ;
    For whilst our pinnace anchors in the Downs,
    Here shall they make their ransom on the sand,   10
    Or with their blood stain this discoloured shore.
    Master, this prisoner freely give I thee,
    And thou that art his mate, make boot of this,
    The other, Walter Whitmore, is thy share.

1.G. What is my ransom, master ? let me know.

91

Master. A thousand crowns, or else lay down your head.
Mate. And so much shall you give, or off goes yours.
Cap. What, think you much to pay two thousand crowns,
And bear the name and port of gentlemen?
Cut both the villains' throats, for die you shall: 20
The lives of those which we have lost in fight
Be counterpois'd with such a petty sum!
1.G. I'll give it, sir, and therefore spare my life.
2.G. And so will I, and write home for it straight.
Whi. I lost mine eye in laying the prize aboard,
And therefore to revenge it, shalt thou die;

                                        To Suffolk

And so should these, if I might have my will.
Cap. Be not so rash, take ransom, let him live.
Suf. Look on my George, I am a gentleman;
Rate me at what thou wilt, thou shalt be paid.   30
Whi. And so am I; my name is Walter Whitmore.
How now? why start'st thou? what, doth death
    affright?
Suf. Thy name affrights me, in whose sound is death.
A cunning man did calculate my birth,
And told me that by water I should die:
Yet let not this make thee be bloody-minded;
Thy name is Gualtier, being rightly sounded.
Whi. Gualtier or Walter, which it is, I care not:

Never yet did base dishonour blur our name,
But with our sword we wip'd away the blot ;   40
Therefore, when merchant-like I sell revenge,
Broke be my sword, my arms torn and defac'd,
And I proclaim'd a coward through the world !

Suf. Stay, Whitmore, for thy prisoner is a prince,
The Duke of Suffolk, William de la Pole.

Whi. The Duke of Suffolk, muffled up in rags ?

Suf. Ay, but these rags are no part of the duke :
[Jove sometime went disguis'd, and why not I ?]   †

Cap. But Jove was never slain, as thou shalt be.

Suf. Obscure and lowly swain, King Henry's blood,   50
The honourable blood of Lancaster,
Must not be shed by such a jaded groom.
Hast thou not kiss'd thy hand and held my stirrup ?
Bare-headed plodded by my foot-cloth mule,
And thought thee happy when I shook my head ?
How often hast thou waited at my cup,
Fed from my trencher, kneel'd down at the board,
When I have feasted with Queen Margaret ?
Remember it, and let it make thee crest-fall'n,
Ay, and allay this thy abortive pride ;   60
How in our voiding-lobby hast thou stood
And duly waited for my coming forth ?
This hand of mine hath writ in thy behalf,

    And therefore shall it charm thy riotous tongue.

Whi. Speak, captain, shall I stab the forlorn swain ?

Cap. First let my words stab him, as he hath me.

Suf. Base slave, thy words are blunt, and so art thou.

Cap. Convey him hence and on our long-boat's side
    Strike off his head.

Suf.   Thou dar'st not, for thy own.

[*Cap.* Yes, Pole.

Suf.   Pole !]

Cap.   Pool, Sir Pool ? lord !   **70**
    Ay, kennel, puddle, sink, whose filth and dirt
    Troubles the silver spring where England drinks.
    Now will I dam up this thy yawning mouth,
    For swallowing the treasure of the realm :
    Thy lips, that kiss'd the queen, shall sweep the ground ;
    And thou that smil'dst at good Duke Humphrey's
        death,
    Against the senseless winds shalt grin in vain,
    Who in contempt shall hiss at thee again :
    And wedded be thou to the hags of hell,
    For daring to affy a mighty lord   **80**
    Unto the daughter of a worthless king,
    Having neither subject, wealth, nor diadem.
    By devilish policy art thou grown great,
    And, like ambitious Sylla, overgorg'd

With gobbets of thy mother's bleeding heart.
By thee Anjou and Maine were sold to France ;
The false revolting Normans thorough thee
Disdain to call us lord, and Picardy
Hath slain their governors, surpris'd our forts,
And sent the ragged soldiers wounded home.   90
The princely Warwick, and the Nevils all,
Whose dreadful swords were never drawn in vain,
As hating thee, are rising up in arms :
And now the house of York, thrust from the crown
By shameful murder of a guiltless king,
And lofty proud encroaching tyranny,
Burns with revenging fire, whose hopeful colours
Advance our half-fac'd sun, striving to shine ;
Under the which is writ ' Invitis nubibus.'
The commons here in Kent are up in arms,   100
And, to conclude, reproach and beggary
Is crept into the palace of our king,
And all by thee.   Away ! convey him hence.

Suf. O that I were a god, to shoot forth thunder
Upon these paltry, servile, abject drudges !
Small things make base men proud : this villain
         here,
Being captain of a pinnace, threatens more
Than Bargulus the strong Illyrian pirate.

Drones suck not eagles' blood, but rob bee-hives:
It is impossible that I should die   110
By such a lowly vassal as thyself.
Thy words move rage and not remorse in me:
I go of message from the queen to France;
I charge thee waft me safely cross the Channel.
Cap. Walter,—
Whi. Come, Suffolk, I must waft thee to thy death.
Suf. *Gelidus timor occupat artus:* it is thee I fear.   †
Whi. Thou shalt have cause to fear before I leave thee.
What, are ye daunted now? now will ye stoop.
1.G. My gracious lord, entreat him, speak him fair.   120
Suf. Suffolk's imperial tongue is stern and rough;
Us'd to command, untaught to plead for favour.
Far be it we should honour such as these
With humble suit: no, rather let my head
Stoop to the block, than these knees bow to any,
Save to the God of heaven, and to my king;
And sooner dance upon a bloody pole,
Than stand uncover'd to the vulgar groom.
True nobility is exempt from fear:
More can I bear than you dare execute.   130
Cap. Hale him away, and let him talk no more.
Suf. Come, soldiers, show what cruelty ye can,
That this my death may never be forgot!

Great men oft die by vile bezonians :
A Roman sworder, and banditto slave   †
Murder'd sweet Tully ; Brutus' bastard hand
Stabb'd Julius Cæsar ; savage islanders
Pompey the Great ; and Suffolk dies by pirates.

Exeunt Whitmore and others with Suffolk

Cap. And as for these whose ransom we have set,
It is our pleasure one of them depart :   140
Therefore come you with us, and let him go.

Exeunt all but the First Gentleman

Re-enter Whitmore with Suffolk's body

Whi. There let his head and lifeless body lie,
Until the queen his mistress bury it.   *Exit*

1.G. O barbarous and bloody spectacle !
His body will I bear unto the king :
If he revenge it not, yet will his friends ;
So will the queen, that living, held him dear.

Exit with the body

SCENE II

Blackheath

{*Enter Bevis and John Holland*}

[*Enter two of the Rebels with long staves*]   †

Bev. Come and get thee a sword, though made of a
lath ; they have been up these two days.

Hol. They have the more need to sleep now, then.

Bev. I tell thee, Jack Cade the clothier means to dress
the commonwealth, and turn it, and set a new nap
upon it.

Hol. So he had need, for 'tis threadbare. Well, I say it
was never merry world in England since gentlemen
came up.

Bev. O miserable age ! virtue is not regarded in handi-
crafts-men.   10

Hol. The nobility think scorn to go in leather aprons.

Bev. Nay, more, the king's council are no good workmen.

Hol. True ; and yet it is said, ' labour in thy vocation ' ;
which is as much to say as, ' let the magistrates
be labouring men,' and therefore should we be
magistrates.

Bev. Thou hast hit it ; for there 's no better sign of a
brave mind than a hard hand.

Hol. I see them ! I see them !   There 's Best's son, the †
    tanner of Wingham,—   21

Bev. He shall have the skins of our enemies, to make
    dog's-leather of.

Hol. And Dick the butcher,—

Bev. Then is sin struck down like an ox, and iniquity's
    throat cut like a calf.

Hol. And Smith, the weaver—

Bev. Argo, their thread of life is spun.

Hol. Come, come, let's fall in with them.

    *Drum.   Enter Cade, Dick Butcher, Smith the Weaver,
            and a Sawyer, with infinite numbers*

Cade. We John Cade, so term'd of our supposed father,—   30

Dick. (*aside*) Or rather, of stealing a cade of herrings.

Cade. For our enemies shall fall before us, inspir'd with
    the spirit of putting down kings and princes,—
    Command silence.

Dick. Silence !

Cade. My father was a Mortimer,—

Dick. (*aside*) He was an honest man, and a good brick-
    layer.

Cade. My mother a Plantagenet,—

Dick. (*aside*) I knew her well, she was a midwife.   40

Cade. My wife descended of the Lacies,—

Dick. (*aside*) She was, indeed, a pedler's daughter, and
  sold many laces.

Smith. (*aside*) But now of late, not able to travel with
  her furr'd pack, she washes bucks here at home.

Cade. Therefore am I of an honourable house.

Dick. (*aside*) Ay, by my faith, the field is honourable,
  and there was he born, under a hedge ; for his father
  had never a house but the cage.

Cade. Valiant I am.   5⁰

Smith. (*aside*) A' must needs, for beggary is valiant.

Cade. I am able to endure much.

Dick. (*aside*) No question of that ; for I have seen him
  whipp'd three market-days together.

Cade. I fear neither sword, nor fire.

Smith. (*aside*) He need not fear the sword, for his coat
  is proof.

Dick. (*aside*) But methinks he should stand in fear of
  fire, being burnt i' the hand for stealing of sheep.

Cade. Be brave, then, for your captain is brave, and vows   6
  reformation.   There shall be in England seven half-
  penny loaves sold for a penny : the three-hoop'd pot
  shall have ten hoops, and I will make it felony to
  drink small beer : all the realm shall be in common,
  and in Cheapside shall my palfry go to grass : and
  when I am king, as king I will be,—

All. God save your majesty !

Cade. I thank you, good people—there shall be no
money, all shall eat and drink on my score, and I
will apparel them all in one livery, that they may   70
agree like brothers, and worship me their lord.

Dick. The first thing we do, let 's kill all the lawyers.

Cade. Nay, that I mean to do.   Is not this a lamentable
thing, that of the skin of an innocent lamb should
be made parchment ; that parchment, being scribbled
o'er, should undo a man ?   Some say the bee stings,
but I say, 'tis the bee's wax ; for I did but seal once
to a thing, and I was never mine own man since.
How now ? who 's there ?

Enter some, bringing forward the Clerk of Chatham

Smith. The clerk of Chatham : he can write and read   80
and cast accompt.

Cade. O monstrous !

Smith. We took him setting of boys' copies.

Cade. Here 's a villain !

Smith. 'Has a book in his pocket with red letters in 't.

Cade. Nay then, he is a conjuror.

Dick. Nay, he can make obligations, and write court-hand.

Cade. I am sorry for 't : the man is a proper man, of
mine honour ; unless I find him guilty, he shall not

die. Come hither, sirrah, I must examine thee: 90
what is thy name?

Clerk. Emmanuel.

Dick. They use to write it on the top of letters: 'twill
go hard with you.

Cade. Let me alone. Dost thou use to write thy name?
or hast thou a mark to thyself, like an honest plain-
dealing man?

Clerk. Sir, I thank God, I have been so well brought up
that I can write my name.

All. He hath confess'd: away with him! he 's a villain 100
and a traitor.

Cade. Away with him, I say! hang him with his pen and
ink-horn about his neck.   *Exit one with the Clerk*

Enter Michael

Mic. Where 's our general?

Cade. Here I am, thou particular fellow.

Mic. Fly, fly, fly!   Sir Humphrey Stafford and his brother
are hard by, with the king's forces.

Cade. Stand, villain, stand, or I 'll fell thee down. He
shall be encountered with a man as good as himself:
he is but a knight, is a'?   11

Mic. No.

Cade. To equal him, I will make myself a knight presently.

(kneels) Rise up, Sir John Mortimer.   *(rises)* Now
have at him !

> *Enter Sir Humphrey Stafford and his Brother,*
> *with drum and soldiers*

Sta. Rebellious hinds, the filth and scum of Kent,
  Mark'd for the gallows, lay your weapons down,
  Home to your cottages ; forsake this groom :
  The king is merciful, if you revolt.

W.S. But angry, wrathful, and inclin'd to blood,
  If you go forward ; therefore yield, or die.   120

Cade. As for these silken-coated slaves, I pass not :
  It is to you, good people, that I speak,
  Over whom, in time to come, I hope to reign ;
  For I am rightful heir unto the crown.

Sta. Villain, thy father was a plasterer,
  And thou thyself a shearman, art thou not ?

Cade. And Adam was a gardener.

W.S. And what of that ?

Cade. Marry, this : Edmund Mortimer, Earl of March,
  Married the Duke of Clarence' daughter, did he not ? 130

Sta. Ay, sir.

Cade. By her he had two children at one birth.

W.S. That 's false.

Cade. Ay, there 's the question ; but I say, 'tis true :
  The elder of them, being put to nurse,

Was by a beggar-woman stolen away,
And, ignorant of his birth and parentage,
Became a bricklayer when he came to age :
His son am I, deny it, if you can.

Dick. Nay, 'tis too true, therefore he shall be king.   140

Smith. Sir, he made a chimney in my father's house, and
the bricks are alive at this day to testify it ; therefore
deny it not.

Sta. And will you credit this base drudge's words,
That speaks he knows not what ?

All. Ay, marry, will we ; therefore get ye gone.

W.S. Jack Cade, the Duke of York hath taught you this.

Cade. (*aside*) He lies, for I invented it myself.
Go to, sirrah, tell the king from me, that, for his
father's sake, Henry the fifth, in whose time boys   150
went to span-counter for French crowns, I am content he shall reign, but I'll be protector over him.

Dick. And furthermore, we'll have the Lord Say's head,
for selling the dukedom of Maine.

Cade. And good reason ; for thereby is England main'd,
and fain to go with a staff, but that my puissance
holds it up.   Fellow kings, I tell you that that Lord
Say hath gelded the commonwealth, and made it an
eunuch : and more than that, he can speak French,
and therefore he is a traitor.   160

Sta. O, gross and miserable ignorance !

Cade. Nay, answer, if you can: the Frenchmen are our
    enemies; go to, then, I ask but this: can he that
    speaks with the tongue of an enemy be a good coun-
    sellor, or no ?

All. No, no, and therefore we 'll have his head.

W.S. Well, seeing gentle words will not prevail,
    Assail them with the army of the king.

Sta. Herald, away, and throughout every town
    Proclaim them traitors that are up with Cade,   170
    That those which fly before the battle ends
    May, even in their wives' and children's sight,
    Be hang'd up for example at their doors :
    And you that be the king's friends, follow me.

            Exeunt the two Staffords, and soldiers

Cade. And you that love the commons, follow me.
    Now show yourselves men; 'tis for liberty.
    We will not leave one lord, one gentleman :
    Spare none, but such as go in clouted shoon ;
    For they are thrifty honest men, and such
    As would (but that they dare not) take our parts.   180

Dick. They are all in order, and march toward us.

Cade. But then are we in order when we are most out of
    order.   Come, march forward.   *Exeunt* 200

SCENE III

Another part of Blackheath

Alarums to the fight, wherein both the Staffords are slain.
Enter Cade and the rest

Cade. Where 's Dick, the butcher of Ashford ?

Dick. Here, sir.

Cade. They fell before thee like sheep and oxen, and thou
behavedst thyself as if thou hadst been in thine own
slaughter-house : therefore thus will I reward thee,
the Lent shall be as long again as it is, and thou shalt
have a licence to kill for a hundred lacking one.

Dick. I desire no more.

Cade. And, to speak truth, thou deserv'st no less. This
monument of the victory will I bear (*putting on Sir*   10
Humphrey's brigandine), and the bodies shall be †
dragged at my horse heels till I do come to London,
where we will have the mayor's sword borne
before us.

Dick. If we mean to thrive and do good, break open the
gaols and let out the prisoners.

Cade. Fear not that, I warrant thee. Come, let 's march
towards London.   *Exeunt*

SCENE IV

London. The palace

Enter the King with a supplication, and the Queen with Suffolk's head, the Duke of Buckingham and the Lord Say

Mar. Oft have I heard that grief softens the mind,
 And makes it fearful and degenerate ;
 Think therefore on revenge, and cease to weep ;
 But who can cease to weep, and look on this ?
 Here may his head lie on my throbbing breast :
 But where 's the body that I should embrace ?

Buc. What answer makes your grace to the rebels'
 supplication ?

King I 'll send some holy bishop to entreat ;
 For God forbid so many simple souls   10
 Should perish by the sword ! And I myself,
 Rather than bloody war shall cut them short,
 Will parley with Jack Cade their general :
 But stay, I 'll read it over once again.

Mar. Ah, barbarous villains ! hath this lovely face
 Rul'd like a wandering planet over me,
 And could it not enforce them to relent,
 That were unworthy to behold the same ?

King. Lord Say, Jack Cade hath sworn to have thy head.

Say. Ay, but I hope your highness shall have his.   20

King. How now, madam ?

Still lamenting and mourning for Suffolk's death ?

I fear me, love, if that I had been dead,

Thou wouldest not have mourn'd so much for me.

Mar. No, my love, I should not mourn, but die for thee.

Enter a Messenger

King. How now ? what news ? why com'st thou in such haste ?

Mes. The rebels are in Southwark ; fly, my lord !

Jack Cade proclaims himself Lord Mortimer,

Descended from the Duke of Clarence' house,

And calls your grace usurper, openly,   30

And vows to crown himself in Westminster.

His army is a ragged multitude

Of hinds and peasants, rude and merciless :

Sir Humphrey Stafford and his brother's death

Hath given them heart and courage to proceed :

All scholars, lawyers, courtiers, gentlemen,

They call false caterpillars, and intend their death.

King. O graceless men ! they know not what they do.

Buc. My gracious lord, retire to Killingworth,

Until a power be rais'd to put them down.   40

Mar. Ah, were the Duke of Suffolk now alive,

These Kentish rebels would be soon appeas'd !

King. Lord Say, the traitors hate thee,
    Therefore away with us to Killingworth.

Say. So might your grace's person be in danger ;
    The sight of me is odious in their eyes ;
    And therefore in this city will I stay,
    And live alone as secret as I may.

          Enter another Messenger

Mes. Jack Cade hath gotten London Bridge :
    The citizens fly and forsake their houses :   **50**
    The rascal people, thirsting after prey,
    Join with the traitor, and they jointly swear
    To spoil the city, and your royal court.

Buc. Then linger not, my lord, away, take horse.

King. Come, Margaret, God our hope will succour us.

Mar. My hope is gone, now Suffolk is deceas'd.

King. Farewell, my lord, trust not the Kentish rebels.

Buc. Trust nobody, for fear you be betray'd.

Say. The trust I have is in mine innocence,
    And therefore am I bold and resolute.   *Exeunt* **60**

SCENE V

London. The Tower

*Enter Lord Scales upon the Tower, walking.   Then enter
two or three Citizens below*

Sca. How now ? is Jack Cade slain ?

1.C. No, my lord, nor likely to be slain ; for they
have won the bridge, killing all those that with-
stand them : the lord mayor craves aid of your
honour from the Tower to defend the city from the
rebels.

Sca. Such aid as I can spare you shall command,
But I am troubled here with them myself ;
The rebels have assay'd to win the Tower.
But get you to Smithfield, and gather head,
And thither I will send you Matthew Goffe ;   10
Fight for your king, your country, and your lives,
And so, farewell, for I must hence again.   *Exeunt*

SCENE VI

London. Cannon Street

*Enter Jack Cade and the rest, and strikes his staff
on London-stone*

Cade. Now is Mortimer lord of this city. And here,
  sitting upon London-stone, I charge and command
  that, of the city's cost, the pissing-conduit run
  nothing but claret wine this first year of our reign.
  And now henceforward it shall be treason for any
  that calls me other than Lord Mortimer.

Enter a Soldier, running

Sol. Jack Cade, Jack Cade !

Cade. Knock him down there.   *They kill him*

Smith. If this fellow be wise, he 'll never call ye Jack
  Cade more : I think he hath a very fair warning.   10

Dick. My lord, there 's an army gathered together in
  Smithfield.

Cade. Come, then, let 's go fight with them : but first,
  go and set London bridge on fire, and, if you can,
  burn down the Tower too.   Come, let 's away.

Exeunt

SCENE VII

London.   Smithfield

*Alarums.   Matthew Goffe is slain, and all the rest.
Then enter Jack Cade, with his company*

Cade. So, sirs ; now go some and pull down the Savoy ;
others to the inns of court, down with them all.

Dick. I have a suit unto your lordship.

Cade. Be it a lordship, thou shalt have it for that word.

Dick. Only that the laws of England may come out of
your mouth.

Hol. (aside) Mass, 'twill be sore law, then, for he was
thrust in the mouth with a spear, and 'tis not whole
yet.

Smith. (aside) Nay, John, it will be stinking law, for his   10
breath stinks with eating toasted cheese.

Cade. I have thought upon it, it shall be so.   Away, burn
all the records of the realm, my mouth shall be the
parliament of England.

Hol. (aside) Then we are like to have biting statutes,
unless his teeth be pull'd out.

Cade. And henceforward all things shall be in common.

Enter a Messenger

Mes. My lord, a prize, a prize ! here 's the Lord Say, which

sold the towns in France; he that made us pay
one and twenty fifteens, and one shilling to the   **20**
pound, the last subsidy.

Enter George Bevis, with the Lord Say

Cade. Well, he shall be beheaded for it ten times. **Ah,**
thou say, thou serge, nay, thou buckram lord!
now art thou within point-blank of our jurisdiction
regal. What canst thou answer to my majesty for
giving up of Normandy unto Mounsieur Basimecu, †
the dauphin of France? Be it known unto thee by
these presence, even the presence of Lord Mortimer,
that I am the besom that must sweep the court clean
of such filth as thou art. Thou hast most traitor- **30**
ously corrupted the youth of the realm in erecting
a grammar school: and whereas before, our fore-
fathers had no other books but the score and the
tally, thou hast caused printing to be us'd, and
contrary to the king, his crown and dignity, thou
hast built a paper-mill. It will be proved to thy
face that thou hast men about thee that usually talk
of a noun and a verb, and such abominable words
as no Christian ear can endure to hear. Thou hast
appointed justices of peace, to call poor men before **40**
them about matters they were not able to answer.
Moreover, thou hast put them in prison, and because

they could not read, thou hast hang'd them, when, indeed, only for that cause they have been most worthy to live. Thou dost ride in a foot-cloth, dost thou not?

Say. What of that?

Cade. Marry, thou ought'st not to let thy horse wear a cloak, when honester men than thou go in their hose and doublets.   50

Dick. And work in their shirt too, as myself for example, that am a butcher.

Say. You men of Kent,—

Dick. What say you of Kent?

Say. Nothing but this; 'tis *bona terra mala gens*.

{*Cade.* Away with him, away with him, he speaks Latin!}

[*Ca.* *Bonum terrum*, zounds, what's that?

Di. He speaks French.

Wi. No, 'tis Dutch.

Ni. No, 'tis Outalian, I know it well enough.]

Say. Hear me but speak, and bear me where you will.
Kent, in the Commentaries Cæsar writ,
Is term'd the civil'st place of all this isle:
Sweet is the country, because full of riches;   60
The people liberal, valiant, active, wealthy,
Which makes me hope you are not void of pity.
I sold not Maine, I lost not Normandy,

Yet to recover them would lose my life.
Justice with favour have I always done,
Prayers and tears have mov'd me, gifts could never.
When have I aught exacted at your hands,
But to maintain the king, the realm, and you?
Large gifts have I bestow'd on learned clerks,
Because my book preferr'd me to the king,   70
And seeing ignorance is the curse of God,
Knowledge the wing wherewith we fly to heaven.
Unless you be possess'd with devilish spirits,
You cannot but forbear to murder me:
This tongue hath parley'd unto foreign kings
For your behoof,—

Cade. Tut, when struck'st thou one blow in the field?

Say. Great men have reaching hands: oft have I struck
   Those that I never saw, and struck them dead.

Geo. O monstrous coward! what, to come behind folks?   80

Say. These cheeks are pale for watching for your good.

Cade. Give him a box o' the ear, and that will make 'em
   red again.

Say. Long sitting to determine poor men's causes
   Hath made me full of sickness and diseases.

Cade. Ye shall have a hempen caudle then, and the help
   of hatchet.

Dick. Why dost thou quiver, man?

Say. The palsy, and not fear, provokes me.

Cade. Nay, he nods at us, as who should say, I 'll be even 90
with you : I 'll see if his head will stand steadier on a
pole, or no.   Take him away, and behead him.

Say. Tell me, wherein have I offended most ?
Have I affected wealth, or honour ? speak.
Are my chests fill'd up with extorted gold ?
Is my apparel sumptuous to behold ?
Whom have I injur'd, that ye seek my death ?
These hands are free from guiltless blood-shedding,
This breast from harbouring foul deceitful thoughts.
O, let me live ! 100

Cade. (*aside*) I feel remorse in myself with his words ; but
I 'll bridle it : he shall die, an it be but for pleading
so well for his life.   Away with him ! he has a
familiar under his tongue, he speaks not a' God's
name.   Go, take him away, I say, and strike off his
head presently, and then break into his son-in-law's
house, Sir James Cromer, and strike off his head,
and bring them both upon two poles hither.

All. It shall be done.

Say. Ah, countrymen ! if when you make your prayers, 110
God should be so obdurate as yourselves,
How would it fare with your departed souls ?
And therefore yet relent, and save my life.

Cade. Away with him, and do as I command ye.

Exeunt some with Lord Say

The proudest peer in the realm shall not wear a head
on his shoulders, unless he pay me tribute ; there
shall not a maid be married, but she shall pay to me
her maidenhead ere they have it : men shall hold of
me in capite ; and we charge and command that their
wives be as free as heart can wish or tongue can tell.   120

Dick. My lord, when shall we go to Cheapside, and take
up commodities upon our bills ?

Cade. Marry, presently.

All. O, brave !

Re-enter one with the heads

Cade. But is not this braver ?   Let them kiss one another ;
for they lov'd well when they were alive.   Now part
them again, lest they consult about the giving up of
some more towns in France.   Soldiers, defer the
spoil of the city until night : for with these borne
before us, instead of maces, will we ride through the   130
streets, and at every corner have them kiss.   Away !

Exeunt

SCENE VIII

Southwark

Alarum and retreat.   Enter Cade and all his rabblement

Cade. Up Fish Street! down Saint Magnus' Corner!
kill and knock down! throw them into Thames!
(*Sound a parley.*)   What noise is this I hear?   Dare
any be so bold to sound retreat or parley, when I
command them kill?

Enter Buckingham and Clifford, attended

Buc. Ay, here they be that dare and will disturb thee:
Know, Cade, we come ambassadors from the king
Unto the commons, whom thou hast misled,
And here pronounce free pardon to them all,
That will forsake thee, and go home in peace.   10

Cli. What say ye, countrymen? will ye relent,
And yield to mercy whilst 'tis offer'd you,
Or let a rabble lead you to your deaths?   †
Who loves the king, and will embrace his pardon,
Fling up his cap, and say 'God save his majesty!'
Who hateth him, and honours not his father,
Henry the Fifth, that made all France to quake,
Shake he his weapon at us, and pass by.

All. God save the king !   God save the king !

Cade. What, Buckingham and Clifford, are ye so brave ?   20
   And you, base peasants, do ye believe him ? will
   you needs be hang'd with your pardons about your
   necks ?   Hath my sword therefore broke through
   London gates, that you should leave me at the
   White Hart in Southwark ?   I thought ye would
   never have given out these arms till you had re-
   covered your ancient freedom : but you are all
   recreants and dastards, and delight to live in slavery
   to the nobility.   Let them break your backs with
   burthens, take your houses over your heads, ravish   30
   your wives and daughters before your faces : for
   me, I will make shift for one, and so, God's curse
   light upon you all !

All. We 'll follow Cade, we 'll follow Cade !

Cli. Is Cade the son of Henry the Fifth,
   That thus you do exclaim you 'll go with him ?
   Will he conduct you through the heart of France,
   And make the meanest of you earls and dukes ?
   Alas, he hath no home, no place to fly to ;
   Nor knows he how to live, but by the spoil,   40
   Unless by robbing of your friends and us.
   Were 't not a shame, that whilst you live at jar,
   The fearful French, whom you late vanquished,

Should make a start o'er seas, and vanquish you?
Methinks already in this civil broil
I see them lording it in London streets,
Crying 'Villiago!' unto all they meet.
Better ten thousand base-born Cades miscarry,
Than you should stoop unto a Frenchman's mercy.
To France, to France, and get what you have lost;   50
Spare England, for it is your native coast:
Henry hath money, you are strong and manly;
God on our side, doubt not the victory.

All. A Clifford! a Clifford! we'll follow the king, and Clifford.

Cade. Was ever feather so lightly blown to and fro as this multitude? The name of Henry the Fifth hales them to an hundred mischiefs, and makes them leave me desolate. I see them lay their heads together to surprise me. My sword make way for   60
me, for here is no staying: in despite of the devils and hell, have through the very middest of you! and heavens and honour be witness, that no want of resolution in me, but only my followers' base and ignominious treasons, makes me betake me to my heels.   *Exit*

Buc. What, is he fled? Go some, and follow him,
And he that brings his head unto the king

Shall have a thousand crowns for his reward.

Exeunt some of them

Follow me, soldiers : we'll devise a mean   70
To reconcile you all unto the king.   *Exeunt*

SCENE IX

Kenilworth Castle

*Sound trumpets.   Enter King, Queen, and Somerset,
on the terrace*

King. Was ever king that joy'd an earthly throne,
And could command no more content than I ?
No sooner was I crept out of my cradle
But I was made a king, at nine months old.
Was never subject long'd to be a king
As I do long and wish to be a subject.

Enter Buckingham and Clifford

Buc. Health and glad tidings to your majesty !
King. Why, Buckingham, is the traitor Cade surpris'd ?
Or is he but retir'd to make him strong ?

Enter, below, multitudes, with halters about their necks

Cli. He is fled, my lord, and all his powers do yield,   10
And humbly thus with halters on their necks,
Expect your highness' doom, of life or death.

King. Then, heaven, set ope thy everlasting gates,
  To entertain my vows of thanks and praise !
  Soldiers, this day have you redeem'd your lives,
  And show'd how well you love your prince and
   country :
  Continue still in this so good a mind,
  And Henry, though he be infortunate,
  Assure yourselves, will never be unkind :
  And so, with thanks, and pardon to you all, 20
  I do dismiss you to your several countries.
All. God save the king ! God save the king !

Enter a Messenger

Mes. Please it your grace to be advertised
  The Duke of York is newly come from Ireland,
  And with a puissant and a mighty power
  Of gallowglasses and stout kernes
  Is marching hitherward in proud array,
  And still proclaimeth, as he comes along,
  His arms are only to remove from thee
  The Duke of Somerset, whom he terms a traitor. 30
King. Thus stands my state, 'twixt Cade and York dis-
  tress'd,
  Like to a ship that, having 'scap'd a tempest,
  Is straightway calm'd, and boarded with a pirate :
  But now is Cade driven back, his men dispers'd ;

And now is York in arms, to second him.
I pray thee, Buckingham, go and meet him,
And ask him what's the reason of these arms.
Tell him, I'll send Duke Edmund to the Tower,
And, Somerset, we will commit thee thither,
Until his army be dismiss'd from him.   40

Som. My lord,
I'll yield myself to prison willingly,
Or unto death, to do my country good.

King. In any case, be not too rough in terms,
For he is fierce, and cannot brook hard language.

Buc. I will, my lord, and doubt not so to deal
As all things shall redound unto your good.

King. Come, wife, let's in, and learn to govern better,
For yet may England curse my wretched reign.

Flourish.   Exeunt

SCENE X

Kent.   Iden's garden

Enter Cade

Cade. Fie on ambition ! fie on myself, that have a sword,
and yet am ready to famish !   These five days have
I hid me in these woods, and durst not peep out,

for all the country is laid for me ; but now am I so hungry that if I might have a lease of my life for a thousand years I could stay no longer. Wherefore on a brick wall have I climb'd into this garden, to see if I can eat grass, or pick a sallet another while, which is not amiss to cool a man's stomach this hot weather : and I think this word 'sallet' was 10 born to do me good : for many a time, but for a sallet, my brain-pan had been cleft with a brown bill ; and many a time when I have been dry, and bravely marching, it hath serv'd me instead of a quart pot to drink in ; and now the word 'sallet' must serve me to feed on.

Enter Iden

Iden. Lord, who would live turmoiled in the court,
And may enjoy such quiet walks as these ?
This small inheritance my father left me
Contenteth me, and worth a monarchy. 20
I seek not to wax great by others' waning,
Or gather wealth I care not with what envy :
Sufficeth that I have maintains my state,
And sends the poor well pleased from my gate.

Cade. Here's the lord of the soil come to seize me for
a stray, for entering his fee-simple without leave.
Ah, villain, thou wilt betray me, and get a thousand

crowns of the king by carrying my head to him:
but I'll make thee eat iron like an ostrich, and
swallow my sword like a great pin, ere thou and   30
I part.

Iden. Why, rude·companion, whatsoe'er thou be,
I know thee not, why then should I betray thee?
Is 't not enough to break into my garden,
And like a thief to come to rob my grounds,
Climbing my walls in spite of me the owner,
But thou wilt brave me with these saucy terms?

Cade. Brave thee? ay, by the best blood that ever was
broach'd, and beard thee too.   Look on me well:
I have eat no meat these five days, yet, come thou   40
and thy five men, and if I do not leave you all as
dead as a door-nail, I pray God I may never eat
grass more.

Iden. Nay, it shall ne'er be said, while England stands,
That Alexander Iden, an esquire of Kent,
Took odds to combat a poor famish'd man.
Oppose thy steadfast gazing eyes to mine,
See if thou canst outface me with thy looks:
Set limb to limb, and thou art far the lesser;
Thy hand is but a finger to my fist,   50
Thy leg a stick compared with this truncheon,
My foot shall fight with all the strength thou hast;

And if mine arm be heaved in the air,
Thy grave is digg'd already in the earth.
As for words, whose greatness answers words,
Let this my sword report what speech forbears.

Cade. By my valour, the most complete champion that
ever I heard! Steel, if thou turn the edge, or cut
not out the burly-bon'd clown in chines of beef,
ere thou sleep in thy sheath, I beseech God on my   60
knees thou mayst be turn'd to hobnails.

Here they fight.   Cade falls

O, I am slain! famine and no other hath slain me:
let ten thousand devils come against me, and give
me but the ten meals I have lost, and I 'ld defy
them all. Wither, garden, and be henceforth a
burying-place to all that do dwell in this house,
because the unconquered soul of Cade is fled.

Iden. Is 't Cade that I have slain, that monstrous traitor?
Sword, I will hallow thee for this thy deed,
And hang thee o'er my tomb when I am dead: 70
Ne'er shall this blood be wiped from thy point,
But thou shalt wear it as a herald's coat,
To emblaze the honour that thy master got.

Cade. Iden, farewell, and be proud of thy victory. Tell
Kent from me, she hath lost her best man, and
exhort all the world to be cowards; for I, that

never feared any, am vanquished by famine, not by
valour.   *Dies*

Iden. How much thou wrong'st me, heaven be my judge.
Die, damned wretch, the curse of her that bare thee;   80
And as I thrust thy body in with my sword,
So wish I, I might thrust thy soul to hell.
Hence will I drag thee headlong by the heels
Unto a dunghill, which shall be thy grave,
And there cut off thy most ungracious head;
Which I will bear in triumph to the king,
Leaving thy trunk for crows to feed upon.   *Exit*

Act Fifth

SCENE I

Fields between Dartford and Blackheath

*Enter York, and his army of Irish, with drum
and colours*

Yo. From Ireland thus comes York to claim his right,
And pluck the crown from feeble Henry's head:
Ring, bells, aloud, burn, bonfires, clear and bright,
To entertain great England's lawful king.

Ah ! *sancta majestas*, who would not buy thee dear ?
Let them obey, that know not how to rule ;
This hand was made to handle nought but gold.
I cannot give due action to my words,
Except a sword or sceptre balance it :
A sceptre shall it have, have I a soul,   10
On which I'll toss the flower-de-luce of France.

Enter Buckingham

Whom have we here ?   Buckingham, to disturb me ?
The king hath sent him, sure : I must dissemble.

Buc. York, if thou meanest well, I greet thee well.

Yo. Humphrey of Buckingham, I accept thy greeting.
Art thou a messenger, or come of pleasure ?

Buc. A messenger from Henry, our dread liege,
To know the reason of these arms in peace ;
Or why thou, being a subject as I am,
Against thy oath, and true allegiance sworn,   20
Should raise so great a power without his leave ?
Or dare to bring thy force so near the court ?

Yo. (*aside*) Scarce can I speak, my choler is so great.
O, I could hew up rocks, and fight with flint,
I am so angry at these abject terms ;
And now, like Ajax Telamonius,   †
On sheep or oxen could I spend my fury.
I am far better born than is the king ;

128

More like a king, more kingly in my thoughts :
But I must make fair weather yet a while,   **30**
Till Henry be more weak, and I more strong.—
Buckingham, I prithee pardon me,
That I have given no answer all this while ;
My mind was troubled with deep melancholy.
The cause why I have brought this army hither
Is to remove proud Somerset from the king,
Seditious to his grace and to the state.

Buc. That is too much presumption on thy part :
But if thy arms be to no other end,
The king hath yielded unto thy demand :   **40**
The Duke of Somerset is in the Tower.

Yo. Upon thine honour, is he prisoner ?

Buc. Upon mine honour, he is prisoner.

Yo. Then, Buckingham, I do dismiss my powers.
Soldiers, I thank you all ; disperse yourselves ;
Meet me to-morrow in Saint George's field,
You shall have pay, and every thing you wish.
And let my sovereign, virtuous Henry,
Command my eldest son, nay, all my sons,
As pledges of my fealty and love ;   **50**
I'll send them all as willing as I live :
Lands, goods, horse, armour, any thing I have,
Is his to use, so Somerset may die.

Buc. York, I commend this kind submission;
    We twain will go into his highness' tent.

Enter King and Attendants

King. Buckingham, doth York intend no harm to us,
    That thus he marcheth with thee arm in arm?

Yo. In all submission and humility
    York doth present himself unto your highness.

King. Then what intends these forces thou dost bring?   60

Yo. To heave the traitor Somerset from hence,
    And fight against that monstrous rebel Cade,
    Who since I heard to be discomfited.

Enter Iden, with Cade's head

Iden. If one so rude, and of so mean condition,
    May pass into the presence of a king,
    Lo, I present your grace a traitor's head,
    The head of Cade, whom I in combat slew.

King. The head of Cade? Great God, how just art Thou!
    O, let me view his visage, being dead,
    That living wrought me such exceeding trouble.   70
    [A visage stern, coal-black his curled locks,
    Deep-trenched furrows in his frowning brow,
    Presageth warlike humours in his life.]
    Tell me, my friend, art thou the man that slew him?

Iden. I was, an't like your majesty.

King. How art thou call'd? and what is thy degree?

Iden. Alexander Iden, that's my name ;
　　　A poor esquire of Kent, that loves his king.
Buc. So please it you, my lord, 'twere not amiss
　　　He were created knight for his good service.
King. Iden, kneel down.　(*He kneels.*)　Rise up a knight
　　　We give thee for reward a thousand marks,　　　　†
　　　And will that thou henceforth attend on us.　　　80
Iden. May Iden live to merit such a bounty,
　　　And never live but true unto his liege !　　　*Rises*
　　　　　　Enter Queen and Somerset
King. See, Buckingham, Somerset comes with the queen :
　　　Go, bid her hide him quickly from the duke.
Mar. For thousand Yorks he shall not hide his head,
　　　But boldly stand and front him to his face.
Yo. How now ? is Somerset at liberty ?
　　　Then, York, unloose thy long-imprison'd thoughts,
　　　And let thy tongue be equal with thy heart.
　　　Shall I endure the sight of Somerset ?　　　　90
　　　False king, why hast thou broken faith with me,
　　　Knowing how hardly I can brook abuse ?
　　　King did I call thee ? no, thou art not king,
　　　Not fit to govern and rule multitudes,
　　　Which dar'st not, no, nor canst not rule a traitor.
　　　That head of thine doth not become a crown ;
　　　Thy hand is made to grasp a palmer's staff,

And not to grace an awful princely sceptre.
That gold must round engirt these brows of mine,
Whose smile and frown, like to Achilles' spear,   **100**
Is able with the change to kill and cure.
Here is a hand to hold a sceptre up,
And with the same to act controlling laws.
Give place : by heaven, thou shalt rule no more
O'er him whom heaven created for thy ruler.

Som. O monstrous traitor ! I arrest thee, York,
Of capital treason 'gainst the king and crown :
Obey, audacious traitor, kneel for grace.

Yo. Wouldst have me kneel ? first let me ask of these,
If they can brook I bow a knee to man.   **110**
Sirrah, call in my sons to be my bail :

Exit Attendant

I know, ere they will have me go to ward,
They 'll pawn their swords for my enfranchisement.

Mar. Call hither Clifford, bid him come amain,
To say if that the bastard boys of York
Shall be the surety for their traitor father.

Exit Buckingham

Yo. O blood-bespotted Neapolitan,
Outcast of Naples, England's bloody scourge !
The sons of York, thy betters in their birth,
Shall be their father's bail, and bane to those   **120**

That for my surety will refuse the boys !

Enter Edward and Richard

See where they come, I'll warrant they'll make it
    good.

Enter Clifford and his son

Mar. And here comes Clifford to deny their bail.

Cli. Health and all happiness to my lord the king !

                                   Kneels

Yo. I thank thee, Clifford : say, what news with thee ?
    Nay, do not fright us with an angry look :
    We are thy sovereign, Clifford, kneel again ;
    For thy mistaking so, we pardon thee.

Cli. This is my king, York, I do not mistake,
    But thou mistakes me much to think I do :   130
    To Bedlam with him ! is the man grown mad ?

King. Ay, Clifford, a bedlam and ambitious humour
    Makes him oppose himself against his king.

Cli. He is a traitor, let him to the Tower,
    And chop away that factious pate of his.

Mar. He is arrested, but will not obey ;
    His sons, he says, shall give their words for him.

Yo. Will you not, sons ?

Edw. Ay, noble father, if our words will serve.

Ric. And if words will not, then our weapons shall.   140

Cli. Why, what a brood of traitors have we here !

Yo. Look in a glass, and call thy image so :
   I am thy king, and thou a false-heart traitor.
   Call hither to the stake my two brave bears,
   That with the very shaking of their chains
   They may astonish these fell-lurking curs :
   Bid Salisbury and Warwick come to me.

Enter the Earls of Warwick and Salisbury

Cli. Are these thy bears ? we 'll bait thy bears to death,
   And manacle the bear-ward in their chains,
   If thou dar'st bring them to the baiting-place.   150

Ric. Oft have I seen a hot o'erweening cur
   Run back and bite, because he was withheld,
   Who, being suffer'd with the bear's fell paw,
   Hath clapp'd his tail between his legs and cried ;
   And such a piece of service will you do,
   If you oppose yourselves to match Lord Warwick.

Cli. Hence, heap of wrath, foul indigested lump,
   As crooked in thy manners as thy shape !

Yo. Nay, we shall heat you thoroughly anon.

Cli. Take heed, lest by your heat you burn yourselves.   160

King. Why, Warwick, hath thy knee forgot to bow ?
   Old Salisbury, shame to thy silver hair,
   Thou mad misleader of thy brain-sick son !
   What, wilt thou on thy death-bed play the ruffian,
   And seek for sorrow with thy spectacles ?

O, where is faith ?   O, where is loyalty ?
If it be banish'd from the frosty head,
Where shall it find a harbour in the earth ?
Wilt thou go dig a grave to find out war,
And shame thine honourable age with blood ?   170
Why art thou old, and want'st experience ?
Or wherefore dost abuse it, if thou hast it ?
For shame, in duty bend thy knee to me,
That bows unto the grave with mickle age.

Sal. My lord, I have consider'd with myself
The title of this most renowned duke,
And in my conscience do repute his grace
The rightful heir to England's royal seat.

King. Hast thou not sworn allegiance unto me ?

Sal. I have.   180

King. Canst thou dispense with heaven for such an
           oath ?

Sal. It is great sin to swear unto a sin ;
But greater sin to keep a sinful oath.
Who can be bound by any solemn vow
To do a murderous deed, to rob a man,
To force a spotless virgin's chastity,
To reave the orphan of his patrimony,
To wring the widow from her custom'd right,
And have no other reason for this wrong,

But that he was bound by a solemn oath?   190

Mar. A subtle traitor needs no sophister.

King. Call Buckingham, and bid him arm himself.

Yo. Call Buckingham, and all the friends thou hast,
    I am resolv'd for death or dignity.

Cli. The first I warrant thee, if dreams prove true.

War. You were best to go to bed, and dream again,
    To keep thee from the tempest of the field.

Cli. I am resolv'd to bear a greater storm
    Than any thou canst conjure up to-day;
    And that I'll write upon thy burgonet,   200
    Might I but know thee by thy household badge.

War. Now, by my father's badge, old Nevil's crest,
    The rampant bear chain'd to the ragged staff,
    This day I'll wear aloft my burgonet,
    As on a mountain top the cedar shows
    That keeps his leaves in spite of any storm,
    Even to affright thee with the view thereof.

Cli. And from thy burgonet I'll rend thy bear,
    And tread it under foot with all contempt,
    Despite the bear-ward that protects the bear.   210

Y.C. And so to arms, victorious father,
    To quell the rebels and their complices.

Ric. Fie! charity, for shame! speak not in spite,
    For you shall sup with Jesu Christ to-night.

Y.C.Foul stigmatic, that's more than thou canst tell.

Ric. If not in heaven, you'll surely sup in hell.

Exeunt severally

SCENE II

Saint Alban's

Alarums to the battle. Enter Warwick

War.Clifford of Cumberland, 'tis Warwick calls :
  And if thou dost not hide thee from the bear,
  Now, when the angry trumpet sounds alarum,
  And dead men's cries do fill the empty air,
  Clifford, I say, come forth and fight with me :
  Proud northern lord, Clifford of Cumberland,
  Warwick is hoarse with calling thee to arms.

Enter York

  How now, my noble lord ? what, all a-foot ?

Yo. The deadly-handed Clifford slew my steed,
  But match to match I have encounter'd him,   10
  And made a prey for carrion kites and crows
  Even of the bonny beast he lov'd so well.

Enter Clifford

War.Of one or both of us the time is come.

Yo. Hold, Warwick, seek thee out some other chase,

For I myself must hunt this deer to death.

War. Then, nobly, York, 'tis for a crown thou fight'st.
As I intend, Clifford, to thrive to-day,
It grieves my soul to leave thee unassail'd.   *Exit*

Cli. What seest thou in me, York? why dost thou
pause?

Yo. With thy brave bearing should I be in love,   **20**
But that thou art so fast mine enemy.

Cli. Nor should thy prowess want praise and esteem
But that 'tis shown ignobly, and in treason.

Yo. So let it help me now against thy sword,
As I in justice and true right express it.

Cli. My soul and body on the action both!

Yo. A dreadful lay!   Address thee instantly.

They fight, and Clifford falls

Cli. La fin couronne les œuvres.   *Dies*

Yo. Thus war hath given thee peace, for thou art still;
Peace with his soul, heaven, if it be thy will!   *Exit*   **30**

Enter young Clifford

Y.C. Shame and confusion! all is on the rout;
Fear frames disorder, and disorder wounds
Where it should guard.   O war, thou son of hell,
Whom angry heavens do make their minister,
Throw in the frozen bosoms of our part
Hot coals of vengeance!   Let no soldier fly.

He that is truly dedicate to war
Hath no self-love ; nor he that loves himself
Hath not essentially but by circumstance
The name of valour.   (*Seeing his dead father*) O, let
  the vile world end,   40
And the premised flames of the last day
Knit earth and heaven together !
Now let the general trumpet blow his blast,
Particularities and petty sounds
To cease !   Wast thou ordain'd, dear father,
To lose thy youth in peace, and to achieve
The silver livery of advised age,
And, in thy reverence, and thy chair-days, thus
To die in ruffian battle ?   Even at this sight
My heart is turn'd to stone : and while 'tis mine, 50
It shall be stony.   York not our old men spares ;
No more will I their babes : tears virginal
Shall be to me even as the dew to fire,
And beauty that the tyrant oft reclaims
Shall to my flaming wrath be oil and flax.
Henceforth I will not have to do with pity :
Meet I an infant of the house of York,
Into as many gobbets will I cut it
As wild Medea young Absyrtus did :   †
In cruelty will I seek out my fame.   60

Come, thou new ruin of old Clifford's house :
As did Æneas old Anchises bear,
So bear I thee upon my manly shoulders ;
But then Æneas bare a living load,
Nothing so heavy as these woes of mine.

Exit, bearing off his father
Enter Richard and Somerset to fight.   Somerset
is killed

Ric. So, lie thou there ;
    For underneath an alehouse' paltry sign,
    The Castle in Saint Alban's, Somerset
    Hath made the wizard famous in his death.
    Sword, hold thy temper ; heart, be wrathful still :
    Priests pray for enemies, but princes kill.   *Exit*   70

Fight.   Excursions.   Enter King, Queen, and
others

*Mar.*Away, my lord ! you are slow ; for shame, away !
*King.*Can we outrun the heavens ? good Margaret, stay.
*Mar.*What are you made of ? you 'll nor fight nor fly :
    Now is it manhood, wisdom, and defence,
    To give the enemy way, and to secure us
    By what we can, which can no more but fly.

Alarum afar off
    If you be ta'en, we then should see the bottom
    Of all our fortunes : but if we haply scape,

(As well we may, if not through your neglect) 80
We shall to London get, where you are lov'd,
And where this breach now in our fortunes made
May readily be stopp'd.

Re-enter young Clifford

Y.C. But that my heart's on future mischief set,
I would speak blasphemy ere bid you fly :
But fly you must ; uncurable discomfit
Reigns in the hearts of all our present parts.
Away, for your relief ! and we will live
To see their day, and them our fortune give :
Away, my lord, away ! *Exeunt* 90

SCENE III

Fields near St Alban's

*Alarum.   Retreat.   Enter York, Richard, Warwick,
and Soldiers, with drum and colours*

Yo. Of Salisbury, who can report of him,
That winter lion, who in rage forgets
Aged contusions, and all brush of time,
And like a gallant, in the brow of youth,
Repairs him with occasion ?   This happy day

   Is not itself, nor have we won one foot,
   If Salisbury be lost.

Ric.   My noble father,
   Three times to-day I holp him to his horse,
   Three times bestrid him ; thrice I led him off,
   Persuaded him from any further act :   **10**
   But still, where danger was, still there I met him,
   And like rich hangings in a homely house,
   So was his will, in his old feeble body.
   But, noble as he is, look where he comes.

       Enter Salisbury

Sal. Now, by my sword, well hast thou fought to-day ;
   By the mass, so did we all. I thank you, Richard :
   God knows how long it is I have to live ;
   And it hath pleas'd him that three times to-day
   You have defended me from imminent death.
   Well, lords, we have not got that which we have : **20**
   'Tis not enough our foes are this time fled,
   Being opposites of such repairing nature.

Yo. I know our safety is to follow them,
   For, as I hear, the king is fled to London,
   To call a present court of parliament.
   Let us pursue him ere the writs go forth.
   What says Lord Warwick ? shall we after them ?

War. After them ! nay, before them, if we can.

Now, by my faith, lords, 'twas a glorious day:
Saint Alban's battle won by famous York   30
Shall be eterniz'd in all age to come.
Sound drums and trumpets, and to London all,
And more such days as these to us befall !   *Exeunt*

Notes

I. i. 232. Althæa, at the birth of her son Meleager, saw the Fates putting a torch in the fire, saying that Meleager's life would last as long as the torch. She snatched it from the fire and preserved it. Later she burned it, and Meleager wasted away. (See, amongst other places, Swinburne's *Atalanta in Calydon*.)

I. ii. 25-31. There is an interesting textual point here. These seven lines are represented in Q 1 by:

> *This night when I was laid in bed I dreamt*
> *That this my staff, mine office badge in court,*
> *Was broke in two, and on the end were plac'd*
> *The heads of the Cardinal of Winchester,*
> *And William de la Pole, first Duke of Suffolk.*

But in Q 3 the passage runs:

> *This night when I was laid in bed I dreamt*
> *That this my staff, my office badge in court,*
> *Was broke in twain, by whom I cannot guess,*
> *But as I think by the Cardinal. What it bodes*
> *God knows; and on the ends were plac'd*
> *The heads of Edmund, Duke of Somerset,*
> *And William de la Pole, first Duke of Suffolk.*

I. ii. 61-69. These lines are represented by three and a half in Q 1:

> *I'll come after you, for I cannot go before,*
> *But ere it be long I'll go before them all,*
> *Despite of all that seek to cross me thus;*
> *Who is within there?*

But Q 3 has:

> *I'll come after you, for I cannot go before,*
> *As long as Gloster bears this base and humble mind:*
> *Were I a man, and Protector as he is,*
> *I'ld reach to the crown, or make some hop headless.*
> *And being but a woman, I'll not behind*
> *For playing of my part, in spite of all that seek to cross me thus.*
> *Who is within there?*

That is to say, that in these two passages Q 3 expands, and in one instance corrects, Q 1 so that the result is nearer to F. I am not clear that the possibly critical nature of this oddity has been sufficiently observed. For what are we to suppose that Jaggard's compositor had in front of him? He was almost certainly setting from a copy of Q 1, or possibly Q 2 (which is no more than a rather careless replica of Q 1). Either, then, he had a corrected copy of Q 1 before him, or he had some sort of a MS., since we can hardly suppose that he made up lines out of his head. If a copy of Q 1, by what had it been corrected? Not I think by the MS., however that MS. had been put together, from which Q 1 had been set, since on examination it seems in the highest degree unlikely that a compositor who had before him a MS. correctly represented by Q 3 could have set it as Q 1. The differences are not of the kind which result from careless composing. And if a MS., what sort of a MS.? For the same reason, not the 'reported' MS. (unless indeed it itself had been corrected subsequently to the printing of Q 1 from it), apart from the comparative improbability of that indifferent MS. having been preserved for twenty-five years. But also not the MS. from which in three years' time F was going to be set, since then we should have instead a rather nearer approximation to F than Q 3 gives us. And in any case, if there was a MS., why do the amplifications of Q 1 'in the direction of' F occur only in two small passages in the second scene of the play? I do not venture to hazard a solution to the problem; that would need a much more careful collation of the texts as a whole than I have been able to conduct; but I wish to suggest that the problem is a real one, and might repay investigation.

I. ii. 82-86. I have given Q 1 here in full, since it is one of the few places in which Q 1 is fuller than F, and not only fuller but probably more dramatic, because more specific. And it suggests that the 'reported text' view does not cover quite all the facts.

I. iii. 78. *She bears a duke's revenues* . . .; another oddity of Q 3. Q 1 has no sign of the line at all; Q 3 inserts something very near to it (*She bears a duke's whole revenues on her back*).

I. iii. 114-17. There is little to choose between the two remarks of Gloucester, but the Queen's retort seems more pointed in Q.

I. iii. 144. *most master*; if the reading is correct the phrase must mean 'the chief master,' *i.e.* the King, and the whole sentence means 'even though she, and not the king, has the regal power, she shall not. . . .' But this is awkward, and Craig is perhaps right in thinking that a line has dropped.

I. iii. 148. *fume*; if it were not for the parallel in *Venus and Adonis*, 316, it would be tempting to cure the metre by reading *fury* (i.e. *furie*, for which *fume* would be an easy graphical error).

I. iv. 39. Here, instead of F's line and a half Q has some picturesque—and Marlowesque—stuff. On the 'foundation-play' view this has to be handled on the lines of 'This is a piece of Marlovian rant that has escaped the reviser' (Hart). On the 'Bad-Quarto' view it implies simply that the actor interpolated a bit of the stuff he was used to. And in fact it rounds off the scene not ineffectively.

I suspect that *sons* in the last line (*sonnes* in Q) is an error for *zounds* (i.e. *souns* or *sounes*).

I. iv. 62. *Aio te . . .*; the traditional answer of the oracle of Apollo to Pyrrhus when he inquired whether he would beat the Romans. In the Latin it can mean either 'I say that you can conquer the Romans,' or 'I say that the Romans can conquer you.'

II. i. 109. The Quarto passage may no doubt be just a bit of gag that was found effective on the stage.

II. ii. 67. The Q passage here, though no doubt hints of it occur elsewhere in F (the rose in I. i. 252 and the bear and ragged staff in V. i. 203), is one of those that makes me suspicious that there are more complications behind the transmission of the text than plain reporting.

II. iii. 11-13. The passage in Q is much better dramatically as a preparation for the Duchess's entry, and avoids the slight awkwardness of *your country*, which turns out to be the Isle of Man.

II. iii. 89. Among the exploits of Bevis of Southampton, one of the favourite heroes of mediaeval romance, was the overthrow of the giant Ascapart, whom he made his squire.

II. iv. 81. *Entreat her not the worse . . .*; cf. *Troilus and Cressida*, IV. iv. 126.

III. i. 114. *my trial-day*; so F. Q reads *the judgement-day*, which is surely much more forcible, since the doit and the groat certainly would be brought against him at his 'trial-day.'

III. i. 192. *are gnarling*; Q reads *stand snarring*.

III. i. 226. *mournful crocodile;* the more usual notion of the crocodile is that 'if he findeth a man . . . he slayeth him, if he may, and then he weepeth upon him and swalloweth him at the last' (Trevisa's translation of Bartholome). But this crocodile is that of Hawkins' voyage of 1565 as narrated by Sparkes: 'His nature is ever when he would have his prey, to cry and sob like a Christian body, to provoke them to come to him, and then he snatcheth at them.'

III. i. 282-83. Instead of these two lines Q reads:

> *The wild O'Neill, my lords, is up in arms,*
> *With troops of Irish kerns, that uncontroll'd*
> *Doth plant themselves within the English pale.*

Cf. Marlowe, *Edward II*:

> *The wild O'Neil with swarms of Irish kerns*
> *Lives uncontroll'd within the English pale.*

On the 'foundation-play' view this, of course, is a piece of Marlowe's work. But surely no writer of Marlowe's competence so nearly repeats himself, and it is much more likely to have been an actor's reminiscence.

III. ii. The staging of this in Q is different and interesting.

> Then the curtains being drawn, Duke Humphrey is discovered in his bed, and two men lying on his breast and smothering him in his bed. And then enter the Duke of Suffolk to them.

Suffolk. *How now, sirs, what, have you dispatch'd him?*

One. *Ay, my lord, he's dead, I warrant you.*

Suffolk. *Then see the clothes laid smooth about him still,*
That when the king comes he may perceive
No other but that he died of his own accord.

Two. *All things is handsome now, my lord.*

Suffolk. *Then draw the curtains again and get you gone,*

And you shall have your firm reward anon.

Exit murderers

Then enter the King and Queen . . .

III. ii. 26. *Nell*; an odd bit of carelessness, repeated by the Queen herself twice in the following speech, where at ll. 100 and 120 we find *Elianor* and *Elinor*.

III. ii. 116. *Ascanius*; the son of Æneas; see *Æneid*, ii., though there it is Æneas himself rather than his son who at the queen's bidding *renovat infandum dolorem* of the fall of Troy.

III. ii. 192. *the bird was dead*; Q reads, more forcibly, I think *the bird came there*.

III. ii. 300. *Mischance and sorrow*; Q reads *Hell-fire and vengeance*.

III. ii. 310. *mandrake*; the mandrake root was supposed to look like a human figure and to shriek when pulled from the ground.

III. ii. 315. *Envy*; one of the seven deadly sins (see *Faerie Queene*, I. iv.). In Golding's *Ovid* we find Envie 'leane as any Rake' living in a 'foul and irksome cave.'

IV. i. (S.D.). For some reason F makes the Captain a Lieutenant.

IV. i. 48. Here, as will be seen, F has to be repaired from the despised Q, as it has again in l. 70.

IV. i. 117. *Gelidus* . . .; the nearest original that has been found is *Aeneid*, vii. 446, *subitus tremor occupat artus*. Before *Gelidus* F mysteriously reads *Pine* (also in italics, as though part of the quotation).

IV. i. 135-38; the errors in the social position or genealogy of the slayers of Cicero, Cæsar, and Pompey are hardly worth pursuing.

IV. ii. (S.D.). It will be noticed that Q gives no names to the rebels. F gives them names which are, one certainly, and the other very probably, names of actors. One J. Holland is given in the cast of the second part of *The Seven Deadly Sins* about 1590. But in Q the rebels take names to themselves as soon as we come to the speech headings, and become George and Nick, and it is worth notice that in the cast mentioned there occurs also a Nick (though of course the name was blackberry-common, and he was there the player of a woman's part).

IV. ii. 20. The Q list of names is much more helter-skelter, though none the less vigorous for that.

> *Why there's Dick the butcher, and Robin the saddler,*
> *and Will that came a wooing our Nan last Sunday, and*
> *Harry and Tom, and Gregory that should have your*
> *Parnill, and a great sort more is come from Rochester,*
> *and from Maidstone, and Canterbury, and all the towns*
> *hereabouts, and we must all be lords and squires, as soon*
> *as Jack Cade is king.*

IV. iii. 11. *brigandine;* the stage-direction is not in the texts, but from Holinshed, and has been generally accepted. But Hart well points out that in Fabyan we have a *sallet* as well as a brigandine, and that in view of IV. x. the sallet would perhaps be more appropriate.

IV. vii. 26. *Basimecu;* this mysterious word is a representation of the French ' baisez mon cul ' and is (*teste* Bradley) still extant in Birmingham in the form *Bozzimecu* as a cheerful insult to organ-grinders. The Q reading is illuminating, *bus mine cue.*

IV. viii. 13. *rabble;* so F, usually emended to *rebel,* perhaps rightly.

V. i. 26. *Ajax;* after the award of Achilles' arms to Odysseus instead of to himself, Ajax went mad and killed sheep and oxen under the delusion that they were his enemies.

V. i. 79. *a thousand marks;* the reward had been announced at

1000 crowns. Henry by generosity, or Shakespeare by carelessness, almost trebled it.   But in Q Henry is even more generous:

> *And for thy maintenance I freely give*
> *A thousand marks a year to maintain thee,*
> *Beside the firm reward that was proclaim'd.*

V. ii. 59, 62. Medea, fleeing from Colchis with Jason, killed her
brother Absyrtus, and threw the body piecemeal overboard to
delay the pursuit.   Aeneas carried his old father Anchises from the
burning ruins of Troy.

Glossary

Many words and phrases in Shakespeare require glossing, not because they are in themselves unfamiliar, but for the opposite reason, that Shakespeare uses in their Elizabethan and unfamiliar sense a large number of words which seem so familiar that there is no incentive to look for them in the glossary. It is hoped that a glossary arranged as below will make it easy to see at a glance what words and phrases in any particular scene require elucidation. A number of phrases are glossed by what seems to be, in their context, the modern equivalent rather than by lexicographical glosses on the words which compose them.

Act First

SCENE I

line

3 PROCURATOR, proxy
28 ALDER-LIEFEST, dearest of all
103 CIRCUMSTANCE, full detail
161 GLOSS, veneer, pretence
167 HOISE, hoist

line

189 PLAINNESS, frankness
HOUSEKEEPING, hospitality
206 MAIN, main business
231 PROPORTION, relation

SCENE II

47 HAMMERING, devising
58 WHEREAS, where

107 SORT, turn out

SCENE III

3 IN THE QUILL, in a body
38 CULLIONS, rascals
81 CALLET, drab
82 MINIONS, favourites
87 QUIRE, choir

87 ENTICING BIRDS, decoy-birds
88 LIGHT, alight
171 FACT, crime
209 DOOM, decision

153

SCENE IV

Act Second

SCENE I

SCENE II

SCENE III

SCENE IV

Act Third

SCENE I

line

51 BEDLAM, lunatic
74 FOND, foolish
    AFFIANCE, trust
91 GEAR, business
105 STAY'D, held back
112, 113 DOIT, GROAT, small coins
126 SHOULD, used to
140 SUSPECT, suspicion
141 CONSCIENCE, instinct
149 PERIOD, end
155 CLOUDY, lowering
160 ACCUSE, accusation
164 LIEFEST, dearest
166 CONVENTICLES, meetings
178 TWIT, blamed
248 EMPTY, hungry
255 POSTED, hurried over
259 CHAPS, jaws
261 QUILLETS, quibbles (*quidlibet*)

line

262 GINS, snares
265 MATES, checkmates
277 TENDER, look after
281 SKILLS, matters
    DOOM, decision
    POST, messenger
282 AMAIN, 'all out'
287 GREEN, fresh
288 EXPEDIENT, immediate
293 FAR-FET, deep
300 CHARACTER'D, marked
310 KERNES, wild Irish soldiers
    (light-armed)
311 TEMPER, moistened
340 TEDIOUS, elaborate
354 FLAW, gust
363 PORPENTINE, porcupine
365 MORISCO, Morris-dancer

SCENE II

20 STRAITER, more strictly
21 OF GOOD ESTEEM, trustworthy
22 APPROV'D IN PRACTICE CULPABLE,
    proved to be involved in
    treasonous plots
52 BASILISK, serpent supposed to
    kill with glance of eye
66 HOLLOW, untrustworthy

83 AWKWARD, contrary
100 PERISH, *active*
111 BE PACKING, 'be off'
112 SPECTACLES, organs of sight
116 WITCH, bewitch
135 RUDE, uncouth
176 LODGED, laid low
178 PROBABLE, full proof

Act III   Sc. ii—*continued*

SCENE III

Act Fourth

SCENE I

SCENE II

Act **IV** Sc. ii—*continued*

line

9 SCORE, reckoning

7 OBLIGATIONS, contracts
COURT-HAND, one of the styles
of Elizabethan handwriting

25 PARTICULAR, individual (*pun on
'general'*)

12 PRESENTLY, on the spot

118 REVOLT, turn back

121 PASS, care

126 SHEARMAN, a shearer of cloth

151 SPAN-COUNTER, pitch and toss

155 MAIN'D, maimed (*old form*)

178 CLOUTED, patched

SCENE III

11 BRIGANDINE, coat of mail

SCENE IV

37 CATERPILLARS, *as agents of destruction* (cf. Joel i. 4)

SCENE VI

3 PISSING-CONDUIT, a small conduit near the Royal Exchange

SCENE VII

33-34 SCORE . . . TALLY, the two halves of the notched stick (kept respectively by debtor and creditor) by which reckonings were kept

45 FOOT-CLOTH, long caparison of horse

53 BONA TERRA MALA GENS, a good land, evil race

70 PREFERR'D ME TO, brought me to notice of

86 CAUDLE, warm drink

119 IN CAPITE, 'in chief,' *i.e.* by direct grant from crown

122 BILLS, pun on (i) bill-hooks, (ii) credit

SCENE VIII

line
20 BRAVE, arrogant
47 VILLIAGO, rascal

line
70 A MEAN, means

SCENE IX

26 GALLOWGLASSES, KERNES, heavy and light armed Irish soldiers

SCENE X

4 LAID, on the watch
8 SALLET, salad
12 SALLET, steel helmet
12-13 BROWN BILL, hooked blade on varnished staff

23 SUFFICETH THAT, it suffices that what
37 BRAVE, challenge

Act Fifth

SCENE I

97 PALMER, pilgrim
153 SUFFER'D, hurt

200 BURGONET, light helmet
215 STIGMATIC, branded deformity

SCENE II

41 PREMISED, foreordained

47 ADVISED, experienced

SCENE III

3 AGED CONTUSIONS, old injuries
BRUSH, blows
4 IN THE BROW OF, wearing the appearance of

22 REPAIRING NATURE, power of recovery